KANG BITCH!

KANG BITCH!

University

BJ Varnado

authorHOUSE®

AuthorHouse™
1663 Liberty Drive
Bloomington, IN 47403
www.authorhouse.com
Phone: 1 (800) 839-8640

Published by AuthorHouse 06/18/2015

ISBN: 978-1-5049-1498-7 (sc)
ISBN: 978-1-5049-1497-0 (e)

Print information available on the last page.

Contents

DEDICATED

To Butter.   Words cannot express!

INTRODUCTION

**Our Mission: Finesse Routines to Give a
Broader Spectrum on Cognitive Actions
Our Motto: Each One *Can* Teach One**

Thank you for choosing **KANG BITCH!** *University.*
Lesson One. *Everything* is Negotiable! You will notice
upon first glance many differences. This is not your usual
brick and mortar higher learning establishment, nor is it
an accredited school. In fact, it's not a school at all, it's a
state of mind. Since it's conception, we have always been
on the cutting edge able to revel in our success by having a
clandestine existence. Our major aspect is "word of mouth",
passing on information learned by women who are willing
to partake in the knowledge of self. Whether you're an
Alpha personality in charge of it all, a demure wallflower
wanting more control of her life, or passively sitting on the
sidelines watching as the world goes by, this course was
designed with you in mind! **KANG BITCH!** *University*
serves a *dual purpose*, business and pleasure. For business,
we'll teach you all the tools of the trade to achieve greatness
to get the all so elusive preverbal brass ring. Executive Status!
A title for women so necessary in today's corporate world.
Lessons will involve stock options, 401k plans, raises, corner
offices, upstart a business etc.. For pleasure in your personal
life, we offer proper etiquette, makeup hints and tips, a
goody bag, how to flirt, and the most important of all, TCB.
With all these tools at your disposal, it won't be difficult to

utilize them both into your busy daily routine. Along with other vital lessons, you will be taught a well kept secret that is NOT to be missed. We'll teach you how to maneuverer it, and win! During this course, we'll also show ways on how to correctly deal with any sticky situations that occur, and how to *solve* them. Contingent on your willingness to adhere to the courses' completion, you will know the true meaning of being an intelligent powerful woman in the "know".

KBU, lovingly called by it's all female alumni, obtains the highest creditability level of academics for Women, as the most greatest form of unconventional education on the planet bar none! Our task is not to empower women, because we feel at **KBU** you've already stood strong on your own facing testicles, I mean *obstacles* in this man's world. As you can see, we don't pull any punches here, so this course is not for the timid, faint of heart, or weak of mind. We don't deceive or bite our tongues. We say what we mean, and mean what we say, then move forward. No slacked-jawed mealy-mouths allowed. No stuttering, stammering, and no holds barred. Just a straight to the point, balls to the wall concept. That's what **KANG BITCH!** *University* is all about. In our first course, **KANG BITCH! #101**, we will be exploring many types of women. Examples below are not limited to...

Women with Power. Multi-millionaires and moneyed women who stand erect on their own or beside a mate. The Woman you *dream* to become.

Legendary Power. Queens of the past that single handedly ruled entire Kingdoms with an iron fist. The Woman you *wish* to become.

KANG BITCH! The Intelligent Woman. The take charge Woman. The aggressive Woman. The ultimate Woman. The Woman you *CAN* become.

Or tuition is not a monetary one. It only consists of your ability to fully succeed in all endeavors. With that said, there aren't any full page media advertisements, glossy panoramic brochures, or pamphlets for your amusement to waste time and money. We don't offer a football team of course, but we do have a lot of balls! However, you will be pleasantly surprised to learn that **KBU** does offer "Nirvana". As an illustrious graduate of **KBU,** you will come to know the true meaning of having it all. Being cognizant of self. You'll be an intelligent Women with Power and have the convictions to succeed and stand tall above them all!

Again, we thank you.

We appreciate you for choosing the *dual purpose,* **KANG BITCH!** *University.*

So...are you ready to get your shit together?

CHAPTER ONE

MEN NEGOTIATE? WOMEN BITCH?

["Dictionary of the Vulgar Tongue," 1811] "BITCH. A she dog, or doggess; the most offensive appellation that can be given to an English woman, even more provoking than that of whore."

A she dog?!? Whore?!? Are you shitin' me? That's their bitch definition, and sadly, it's what some men think of us. For no other reason, it's meant to disrespect and demean. When the word bitch is used in the above terminology, of course it is vulgar. When a man calls us bitch, it's done for cruel intent and purposes. *But,* to some women, we consider it as a term of endearment, and come to embrace it when speaking to our girl friends. No harm is meant or implied when we say, "Whassup bitch!" Or, "C'mon bitch, I gotta pick up the kids!" *Or,* "Bitch you wearin' dem shoes/dress/outfit!" I remember when speaking to one of my oh so fabu friends, sporting a stunning bright fuchsia boa that only he can pull off, and looking absolutely amazing. The words "BRAVA BITCH*!" had been uttered. But when a man or woman calls us *bitch* in anger, all bets are off! I don't know about you, being the Taurus that I am, I see red*. My face gets hot, vision is blurred, and I start speaking as if I had Tourette Syndrome! I'm like a bull in a china shop and anybody standing in my path had better look out. I love the word for what it *could* mean, but hate the word for what has *come* to mean in our society. It's a love/hate relationship… sort of like with men. Confusing? I'll explain.

Please allow me to state this so there's no confusion. This is not some type of male bashing, men aint shit, all of you men are all alike, I can do bad all by myself, I don't need a man to validate my well being or self-worth, my daddy told me don't take no shit off no man or any of the other trifflin' ass bullshit colloquiums we come up with to feel better about our short comings kind of book. It is quite the opposite. It's to help you to better understand *you* in this man's world. Yes my pretties, I said this *man's* world. The sooner you wrap your mind around that key fact, the easier it would be for you to operate, maneuver and succeed in his world. Remember baby, it's *his* world, you're just a squirrel trying to get a nut…preferably his! In these lessons of **KANG BITCH! # 101** ladies, we're turning the tables on men, but adding a pretty lace tablecloth to soften the blow!

Now that we've got that straight, we'll resume.

Men negotiate. Women bitch. Oh really now?!? Who in the **hell** said that? You know who, the powers that be. The chauvinist males! Oh, didn't know that word *chauvinist* existed anymore? Well it does, to the die hard "good 'ol boys" and to those in the corporate world the word is alive, well and breeding like junk yard dogs! Let's start at the beginning. It's very simple. Men and women are different. Duh! "I *know* that", you say. It doesn't take a rocket scientist to figure that out. Ok, let's see what they really "negotiate". Just think about it for a moment. Suga, the men have been talking about it, thinking about it, and hockin' it for years! Know what it is? Sex! Sex! Sex!

SEX. Used in every avenue, every venture, and every preconceived notion their little brains can muster. They even use it in their advertising. Why do you think they need a coquettish, pouty lipped, daisy duke wearing, bust heaving, secret sauce dripping down her arm model to sell a damn fast food sandwich? Because they *think* it's sexy. We *all* know the secret behind the sexual innuendo "sauce". C'mon! Is that *really* necessary? They use it in constructing. The Washington Monument standing tall and erect, and the Cruise Missile's obvious penis like form. Sex was even used during warfare. During World War ll, scantly clad(for the time)vixens were painted on their planes to adorn them. Negotiation? What are they negotiating here, a little T & A? Even something as simply as an innocent cleansing, youths in the boys gym shower, measure each other's virility by the size of their penis to determined manhood. Wow, *that's* maturrrre! Like notches on a belt in a cowboy movie of the wild, wild West, the more conquest, the bigger the man. Somebody get a rope! Or, in one final hurrah at a bachelor party, it's use to close a chapter on one part of their life to enter into another. It's sex, sex, sex! Always has been, always will be. They've been thinking outside the proverbial *furry box* so to speak, working their plans, putting it in motion, running it up the flag pole, fighting battles, winning and losing wars over it, and lives lost because of it. In the days of King Lear, chastity belts were constructed to protect future heritages from being tainted by outside seed. Boundaries setup, territories formed, guns drawn, dowries given. Now tell me, what does that sound like they(under the guise of negotiations)are doing? You know what it is…you're thinking of it right now! Ok, ok, I'll back off for now. I'm asking too much of you too soon and you're not there yet. Or, you're a little too pooh-pooh to say it. Hell, I'm not! Sounds like men are protecting the pussy! Men have had the wealth, power and control for eons for only one reason*.

Here are two examples of men with power. I show them as examples so you'll see what you might have to encounter along the way. The quintessential players, that are the true to the Game*. But don't be intimidated ladies, they *all* put their pants on the same way!

According to Forbes 2012, a Nigerian Business Magnate Aliko Dangote is worth $11.2 billion as the world's wealthiest black person. In March 2011, also according to Forbes they estimated the more well known Donald Trump's net worth to be $2.7 billion.

Not to say that we don't have women to be proud of. We do. *Multi-billionaires!* Ms. Oprah, as we know is very near and dear to us, definitely has the Midas touch when it comes to business. But there might be one you may or may not know of. Drum roll please! THE richest woman in the world worth a staggering **$3.2 billion!** She is Africa's 61 year old Ms. Folorunsho Alakji. She owns at least $100 million in real estate and owns a $46 million private jet. She is beautiful! She is rich! She is Black! Bet girlfriend's shoe collection is outrageous!

How did they get from subservient, to Women with Power and in the "know?" Ms. Oprah certainly didn't start off that way, neither did any other women with power. What do they know that we don't? Is there really a key to success*? There's not some magic potion we could drink, because if it was, we'd be chugging the shit by the gallon! Could it be subtle changes in our lives must be made in order to succeed? Eureka! I've got it! Pay close attention to what men **SAY.** Unknowingly, they will give you the answer to the question!

Men <u>NEGOTIATE.</u> Women *bitch.*

<u>NEGOTIATE</u> both sides of you, business **and** pleasure. Basically, to negotiate means to get as close as possible to a solution that is satisfactory for both sides. Opt for new ways to *enhance* your business side, and new ways to *increase* your pleasure side. Get rid of that ho-hum comfort-zone lazy attitude and whining. Don't let anyone fool you, we know full well how to negotiate without bitching or being one! It's a part of our everyday life as much as breathing, we do it without even thinking. Shopping around for bargains at the mall, supermarket, yard sales, couponing, refereeing the kids, rationalizing with your mate etc., the list goes on and on. The only reason men say we bitch, and they negotiate, is we get **emotional** when dealing in business. We *are* more emotional, it's a part of our nature, but ladies, we have to learn to control these emotions more. Keep them in check *if* we want to succeed in business. Men are expecting us to fold when the going gets tough or once confronted, so turn the tables. Lesson One. *Everything is Negotiable!* It's time

to forgo those damn cotton granny drawls and don some pretty sexy red* panties. Notice I didn't say black, pink or even white panties. No baby, RED! The color RED is empowering. It means: BEWARE! LOOK OUT! TAKE NOTICE! Break out you're your Diva Style. Time to flip the script, and woman the fuck up. Time for a new **you!**

Just to let you know, this book intertwines. I'm here to help not to confuse. Noticed the*? I will leave a little breadcrumb* to let you know we are going to discuss a topic further. The tips, guidelines, and playful scenarios are easy to follow. It will teach you how to deal with problems, and manage difficult situations. It'll also teach how you to always be prepared, think on your feet and hit the ground running.

Scenario. You didn't have time to do laundry and you've gotten down to the "ugly" clothes. You need some wine 'cause its been a fucker of a day and you want some *me* time. So you decide to make a run to the corner liquor store. You throw on some shit lying on the floor/chair you wouldn't be caught dead in any other time, jump in the car, run in the store and as fate would have it, you see a *really* cute guy/girl(hey, I don't judge). "SHIT! SHIT!", you say under your breath looking down at your hideous outfit. He/she is interested, smiles, walks closer to you looking fine as wine, and smelling like a warm summer breeze. You, scratching your uncombed head as if you had fleas, looking like dammit to hell. What do you do?

End Scenario

Well the jig is up! You look like something the dog threw up... ate ...and threw up again! Your hair is a mess, your clothes probably need ironing, no make up, you look like an unmade bed and even less appealing. Shame, shame, shame on you!!! Don't worry my love, I'm here to help, not to judge.

Solution: Ok, you can't fix broke, the damage is done. There is no genie that is going to magically appear, make this train wreck that is you, all better. Time for a little collateral damage control. He/she sees you, you see them that's been established. Stand up, stick your chest out, but DON'T overdo it, greet the person with a blush of a smile. Once the conversation begins, apologize for your appearance by saying you've been ill with the flu, but feeling better now, and this is the first time you've been out. **Make sure to say you're feeling better because you want to date this person. Soon!** *Don't babble* on about your kids, your job, the neighbors, your parents, or the man on the moon. Save that for your second meet. This conversation is strictly about you two, so be precise. Ask for their assistance to help you find the chicken soup, orange juice, whatever goes along with cold/flu runny nose, snot, phlegm, decongestant, whatever, make it up as you go along ...remember you are much too weak and much too sick to do this on your own, but well enough to receive a visitor(If he's a gentleman, he'll show up at your door bearing gifts)besides men love taking care of women. Make sure you are standing next to him while checking out, do some small talk. Comment on the weather, his outfit, his hair, then cough and an occasional sneeze while "accidently" grabbing his arm to hold onto for balance, this adds a nice touch. *Buy* the items, give him your number. Go to *another* store to purchase your wine. Whew! Disaster averted. Now, get down on your pathetic, ashy knees and pray to whatever Higher Power(God, Allah, Buddha, Gucci)you believe in and vow to never leave the house unpretty again! **End Solution.**

Drama like this in your personal life may or may not happen, but at least you have options. The scary part there is a strong possibility it *could* happen! This puts you in the line of danger, and committing *the* worse offense of all. Character Assignation*. Remember to think on your feet, be able to hit the ground running, and don't ever be caught off guard. It's all about being prepared*, because the same scenario applies in your business life. What if he had been a potential high-end client you've been chomping at the bit to get? You've tried everything to set up a meet with this client for weeks! All you got was the cold shoulder from his overly protective, nothing gets pass me, the buck stops here, I know for a **fact** he would not be interested in this, his calendar is full for the next three to four weeks Administrative Assistant*. He knows of your portfolio, because you've manage to negotiate it pass Madam gate keeper from hell watchful eye with another staff person in his office. He recognizes you. He's walking towards you. You, looking like dammit to hell! What do you do?

Solution: The above solution applies!

Want to know why? 'Cause he's a man. It's all about sex! Wrap your mind around it. Embrace it. Bottom line, we have the pussy, they want the pussy, *you* are in control queen! Sex it's always on their mind. Don't look at me all cross-eyed,

I didn't make up the rules* to this damn game*! But I do know *where* they like to play! In or out the boardroom, in a restaurant, in a bar, in a grocery store, in your house, in my house, inside, outside, on a table, on the floor, in an alley, a slow grind against the wall, throw me down and take it daddy, on a car roof, on the hood, in the back seat, on the trunk, on the kitchen table/counter, you on top, me on top, on your/my side, 69, missionary, doggy style, standing up, sitting down, in his lap, backwards, forwards, legs on shoulders*, feet on walls, sensuous thighs writhing, suck his dick like your mad at it, engulfing, pulsating, tight wet pussy* around throbbing dick in pussy, in and out going deep in between the sheets! Baby he's a man, with dog tendencies.

According to the Urban dictionary: *Dog. A guy who hits and runs, as in he tells girls what they wanna hear to get in their panties and as soon as he gets the pussy, he's gone. Unable to commit to one woman. Dog.*

In some black vernaculars, did you know they refer to each other as *dawgs?* As you know a dog will fuck anytime, anywhere...and yet, *I'm* the bitch!? In fact, they greet each other as "dawgs". You've heard them. "Whassup dawg? Or, I'll be back baby, Imma hang wit my dawg today." Not to say that black men or any men are dogs but....Wait a minute Mr. Man, let me try to wrap my mind around your little pearls of wisdom. You say, 'Men negotiate, women bitch', because when men get together, important issues are settled. Women get together, we gossip. The male of the specie "dawg." Female, is *automatically* a "bitch". Do I have that right? Oh. Ok. Now I get it?

It's got to be a reason why men think this way. Maybe it's some kind of territorial marking, boundary setting, pissin' on trees* bullshit. I'm not here to try and figure them out, I just want to *understand*. Once you understand the male psyche, half the battle is won. The other half is satisfying their ego*, needs, wants, desires, you know, fuck 'em well. Now I'm not saying to go out there hike up your skirt and sell your cupcake to the highest bidder...although, I have been giving some thought to pen a new book in the very near future titled, **"Pussy, *STILL* Profitable in the New Millennium"**...just kidding! But, if you are serious about winning, you must be on point, open for business, and ready to hit the ground running every time you walk your fabulous diva ass out the door! Men know this, we knew it too, but somewhere down the line we forgot it, lost it, or simply were not taught it. Can you imagine living the life our moms lived with their ways of thinking? The thought of a woman's place is in the home, and the best way to a man's heart*, is through his stomach. Ugh! I think I'm going to throw up! Walking around the house in heels and pearls cooking and cleaning all day looking like Donna Reed! Although I think that's a fabulous look, that would be fine *if,* **I stayed home all day!**

My mother taught me to stay in a woman's place. God rest her soul, I love my mother and that was fine for *her* time. The values she taught me still rings true, but in this day and age, I don't believe *every* woman's place is in the home.

Ladies, this is your wake-up call, time to stand up! After all, aren't you like me? I'm an educated Professional Business Woman! I have an intelligent finger on the pulse of society, with up to date world views. I am erect standing make my *own* money having Gucci wearing Prada buying Tiffany's loving kind of woman! And dammit, I don't believe none of that bullshit…unless your plan is to *be* Donna Reed. I feel that after a hard day at the office with spreadsheets fax machine breaking down running out of toner no lunch hot flashes fuckin' pseudo cramps putting out fires left and right *and*, the idiot that's in charge of the whole department sent me on a wild goose chase that only ended five minutes before it was time for me to go home. Jump in the car finally have some me time, the car is almost on empty, drive to gas station get gas because **he** didn't fill it when **he** used it the last time, go to cleaners then to the drug store for **his** prescription. Now **he** wants dinner? After the day I've had, that *bitch* can make his own peanut butter and jelly sandwich for all I care or pick up something on his way back to **his** house. And so far as a woman's place is in the home, baby you don't want my ass pinned up in a house all day with nothing to do but housework. Shit, I'm an educated Professional Business Woman! I have an intelligent finger on the pulse of society…...! What the **fuck** am I gonna do make jam?! Sew?! Knit?! Paint the kitchen?! Yeah right. Wanna see me bitch, and NOT negotiate? Ask me to serve you dinner after the day I've had! Look, if I can find a man that is willing to go out and make the bacon, take out the trash *and*, mow the lawn*, I'll be happy to fry it up in the pan. That door swings *both* ways. It's a new day Donna, time to woman the fuck up!

We must shed those archaic ways of thinking. Wrap your mind around it, embrace it. It's their mantra, let it be yours. Say it with me ladies. SEX SELLS! We've got to get all our ducks* in a row, dot all our I's, and cross all our T's. Start from square one to build a strong foundation*. Erase all the idiotic notions we were given about not being good enough or only good for one thing, laying on our backs, barefoot and pregnant, or being the weaker sex. We are not the weaker sex. Listen, if men had to endure the pain of labor, we'd be a population of males! Show them we don't bitch, *we* too can negotiate! The good 'ol boys in their ivory towers think women are incapable of negotiating without bitching. They want us out of their precious club because we don't *think* as they do. Maybe they're wish is for us to be more like them, more apt in the ways of business.

There's an old saying, "Be careful what you wish for, you just might get it." On that note, I'd like to pose a question to the men.

Ever wonder what happens when you organize a bitch*?

CHAPTER TWO

TOOLS OF THE TRADE

Organization: Having order. Creating standards or rules. Having purpose or system. Get on the good foot ladies, we're about shake this up and do some much needed housekeeping. As with all things we want to freshen up, with our *Life Style Change* we need to do some serious self cleansing. Don't get scared, I'm not talking enemas, but getting rid of old shit is crucial. We need to start our diet by tossing out the old, to get ready for the new. Pay attention. The next few chapters are a quick crasher course in the tools and techniques you will need in your daily lives. Refer back when you need to, highlight it, bookmark it, take a picture of it, commit it to memory. Do whatever necessary so you don't forget it. We mere peons aren't lucky or rich enough, *yet* to have a full staff glam team to greet us each morning as we awake from Le boudoir*, but we still can manage to stumble our way into the bathroom for our daily routine. Each example is simple, but must be completed and *kept enforced* once you begin.

REMEMBER: IF YOU LEAVE THE HOUSE, DON'T SKIP IT!!!!!!!

Clothes. Must be freshly washed. No holes, loose threads, stains etc. Needs ironing…iron it…don't want to iron it… wear something else!

Makeup. Nothing fancy. There's no need to go overboard or overspend when buying cosmetics. Make a mad dash to your local drug store CVS Walgreen Rexall whatever. I know Wal-Mart is cheaper but if you go in with the *one* thought of just buying cosmetics you WILL overspend! You know how we do. Oooo this is cute I didn't know they had this color. Or, these would look good with my....C'mon girl, stay focus! Get a compact powder one closest to your own coloring, and lipstick, red of course. There's many hues of red to choose from, get a shade you are comfortable with.

Helpful hint: You can also use lipstick as rouge on your cheeks! Just dab once on each cheekbone and blend gently in a circular motion. Viola! Instant blush.

Nails. Don't have time/money for manicure. Get a bowl of warm water and add a drop or two of dawn or any dishwashing liquid you have on hand. With an old toothbrush, gently scrub underneath nails to clean out dirt. Rinse, dry completely. Trim nails just above the finger. Apply one(1)coat of clear polish followed by one(1)shade of red you like, then two(2)top coats of clear polish. *Let nails dry completely before doing anything!* This "kitchen table" method should last about a week, and will do nicely in a pinch(or if money is tight)especially if you're getting ready for a meet with MONEY* in the next day or two. But please, have them done professionally *before* your next meet. **IMAGE*** is *everything.*

Hands. Moisturize. Moisturize. Moisturize. At night, slather on a good cocoa butter lotion. Choose one that isn't oily and apply daily and often. Rub them together really fast to warm and distribute lotion deep into skin front *and* back of hands. You'll be greeting and shaking hands with MONEY and nothing says WELCOME like a pair of warm soft subtle hands!

Shoes. Say it with me ladies. If I *leave* the house, no damn **FLIP FLOPS*! HOUSE SHOES!** or **SLIPPERS!** Acceptable: Any form, fashion or color of closed in or open toed cute leather strappy sandals with baubles tassels beads feathers(no bells)that dance every time you take a step. Even mules or espadrilles are quite comfortable. Flats, with a slight heel, or tennis shoes if you have a lot of errands running around with the kids. Or if like me, are a true Diva, and being glam is *always* at the top of your list, Brava Bit...oops sorry, do heels! If it's Spring/Summer and a dress or skirt is in order, don't forget to wax/shave your legs *and* thighs, and polish those tootsies a bright red my queen!

NOTE: Flip flops can only to be worn on the beach, with *your* kids, with *your* Sweetie, with *your* friends on *your own* time. Change to slip-on shoes*, if you run in the store or send Sweetie. If you're just getting chips and ice, etc. send the kids, that's what they are there for. House shoes/slippers are to be worn in *your* house!

PURSE. Lipstick, lotion, hand sanitizer, compact, Visine/clear eyes eye drops etc. baby wipes a *nice* ink pen business cards cell phone **ONE** credit/debit card ID and only $5.00 to 10.00 in cash. Nothing else should be carried in your purse. The first 6 items are to keep yourself beautified and refreshed. The next is for business. We make the mistake of taking 5, 6, or 7 credit/debit cards with us everyday when all we use is one. We run the risk of losing or stolen only to have the time consuming task of having them replaced. The cash is for parking meters to buy gum or change for someone helpful carrying bags to the car.

CAR/TRUNK Under front seat, keep an extra pair of slip-on shoes. GOODY BAG: In trunk *at all times*. Keep a dark blue/black carryall bag containing, roll on deodorant, small bottle of fragrant lotion, mouthwash, tooth paste/brush comb/brush, compact, faux diamond-stud earrings. Tennis shoes, white socks, sweats w/hood, animal print underwear/matching bra. Once used, wash clothes and return all items to trunk.

GLOVE BOX. Current car insurance/registration papers, auto repair log, flashlight. DO NOT keep anything in your car with home address on it. If it does, buy a black felt tip pen and black it out. Don't have one, buy one. Mace or any spray bottle(adjust nozzle to pinpoint spray)filled with water and any eye irritant like liquid soap, chili peppers, hot sauce to ward off attackers.

CONSOLE. Listen to something inspirational. Or get a tape to learn a second or third language. Play some soothing jazz. Chew bubble gum. Do whatever floats your boat to relieve stress* while you drive....but no cell phones allowed!

GOODY BAG: *SEE* CAR/TRUNK *Mini Scenario.* You are invited to Sweetie's house for a sumptuous dinner prepared by his own loving hands. Dinner is over, you're sipping a cognac when he gets amorous. The evening has now turned into *A Night Maneuver.* Do you have your Goody Bag? *Every* woman must have a 'Goody Bag'.

A NIGHT MANEUVER: A night maneuver can occur when you are out with your girls, unexpectedly, you see Sweetie with his boys. He invites you back to his place for a little coochie-coo after you are finish partying. Now this can be an all nighter event…if you're lucky! *Or*, it starts out as an 8p.m dinner at your man's house, you're looking fabulous in an after five black sequined floor length evening gown, hair coiffed, makeup impeccably done, glam bam thank you ma 'me head to toe. It's now **10:30a.m.** and you must leave. What do you do?

Without the proper attire, the neighbors in his now wide awake, busy "Those people are always in my business", you've heard him say on a numerous occasions, hustle bustle, condo complex, including the doorman, will know you've been a naughty girl, and you'll have to make that walk of shame to your car. This is *not* the time for you to say let them think what they want to think, I'm a grown ass woman. You *are* a grown ass woman with one exception. You are a grown ass *Professional Business Woman*, because *image** is *everything.* Potential clients are everywhere, he could be your man's next door neighbor! Remember *you* are the live billboard advertisement for your business. Potential MONEY is always out there, and you only have one chance to make a good first impression. A Diva Style must be prepared* at *all* times.

Have Sweetie to retrieve your goody bag from your car(if he picks you up, remember to transfer your goody bag to his car)take a shower, stash dress, shoes, etc. in goody bag. Put on items in bag. Don't zip jacket completely, allow a portion of the pretty animal print bra to show, but pull up the hood to cover your hair, because by now, I'm positive it isn't *coiffed*. Now, if you must leave, it *looks* like you're off to the gym for a workout, and just stop by Sweetie's for a little kiss. If he drove, it *looks* like he forgot something back at his condo, and you just went up with him to use the facilities before he drops you off at the gym. That's you're story, so stick with it if you happened to bump into MONEY on your way out!

Oh, wondering about the pretty animal print bra set? That's for you Boo, to *feel* power 'cause you get this right, you are one wild cat* sexy beast! A woman who incorporates these traits into her new diet of *Life Style Change* will know the full meaning of having it all. It's all about being prepared. You **must** be prepared *at all times.*

Simple rule of thumb…

A woman wanting to **operate** in this man's world must be prepared for anything at any given time. She has to have a plan A, B, and C.

A woman wanting to **win** in this man's world must be prepared for anything at any given time. She has to have a plan A, B, C, D, E, F, G, H, I, J, K, L, M,…….

This formula is pretty much self explanatory if you're an intelligent woman. If you don't get it, no amount of explanation would suffice.

CHAPTER THREE

THE GAME

Men are visual creatures*. *Breathe this, live this, commit it to memory.* If you hold a baby on your lap, and you're wearing a pair of dangling bright sparkly earrings, that little scamp will make a bee line for them quicker than you can bat an eye. Same with a man! Laughable but true, they are like babies when they see glittering objects. It's called "Shiny Ball Syndrome". When choosing an outfit for a meet with a client or a date, wear a pair of earrings that dazzle and shine every time your head moves. Careful not to choose a pair that's too large or makes too much noise. Men are very easily distracted. Their attention can be interrupted by a crumb on the table! Away from you, what you're saying *and* what you're doing. Sadly, a lot of women don't even *know* there's a game going on, let along how to play or what the rules and regulations are. I know! They're many complex segments to 'The Game'. Break out the lace tablecloth. Light 'em if you got 'em!

Scenario. A well dressed, well groomed man walks into a conference room full of equally well dressed well groomed men. You, the only female in the room, standing by the buffet table, also well groomed and dressed accordingly. He works the room. Confident, aggressive, while people vie for his attention. Group after group of men he greets, he smiles, being pleasant, shaking hands, and making small talk. Every now and then, the well dressed well groomed man lets out a manly laugh as they do, and moves to the next set of men. Finally, he sees you, nods, and moves on... without saying a word! Huh? What just happened!?!

End Scenario

Solution. Well for one thing, he probably thought you were part of the wait staff! It doesn't matter how *dressed accordingly* you are. If you are not willing to get down there in the trenches, get your hands dirty with the rest of the pack of wolves, you might as well tend tables! Not that there's anything wrong with that profession, and you can make a decent living, but we are not talking making a **decent** living. We are talking CAREERS! HUGE FUTURES! STOCK OPTIONS! Fuckin 401k's! CORNER OFFICES! VACATIONS IN BIMNI! Shit if you can get that while serving tables, I'll put in my application at Denny's right now and call it a damn day! It's part of the Game*. Lose it, bye-bye go home! Win it, BUY a home!

This is The Game. The well kept secret known only to an Elite few. Time to play. Time to *win!* Losers lose poorly, and winners can win it all. The man that walked into the conference room is *your* MONEY, *your* bread and butter. MONEY belongs to **you,** he just doesn't know it yet. I don't care if there's a room full of suits, well dressed or otherwise, act as if this is *your* man and these other suits are bitches that want to **take** *your* man. You know what to do, tell them they had better step off by your actions! Be a mad dog with a bone. Stand up to your opponent* face to face. Be forceful, and aggressive. Size them up*. You are not part of the wait staff, or part of the prey*. You're a wild cat. Step your ass away from that buffet table dammit. A wild cat hunts better on an empty stomach, and I want you **hungry!** You should already be keeping an eye out for MONEY even before he comes in the front door, so position yourself there. Make yourself ready to receive MONEY. How do you look? Your hair. Makeup. Any out of place? Does it need a touch up? Hands. Make sure your hands are warm, soft and moisturized. If not, make a mad dash to the ladies room for repairs. Run some warm water on your hands and dry them completely. There's nothing worse than shanking hands with someone with clammy hands! Don't have time to run to ladies room? Freshen hands with baby wipes from your purse and let air dry. Rub vigorously to warm.

The purse you carry is very important. It should be a small one that has a shoulder strap, *never a clutch,* because you want to keep both hands free. In it carry(one)car key(one) house key, your business cards and a NICE pen. If you have one with your name or Company's logo even better, compact, red lip stick, small comb/brush baby wipes, small lotion, breath mints and ID. NOTHING ELSE. As soon as you see MONEY, introduce yourself by extending your hand first. You must look MONEY **directly in his eyes, to keep and hold his attention***. Then drop some little tidbit about his company you researched online the night before and tell MONEY how you can improve his bottom line while *still* gently holding MONEY's hand. Keep it direct. Keep it simple. He will try to get away at this point, because men's attention span is short if its not a naked woman standing in front of him, or sports related, but don't let him get away without giving him your business card, or Company's logo pen. Before MONEY walks away, tell MONEY in your most soft sensuous alluring voice how much you are looking forward to seeing him again, flutter them eyes*, and smile, baby! SMILE!

There's much more to the Game*, which we will delve into deeper as we progress. For now, I want to switch gears for a moment, and discuss lies. We all tell them men and women alike, but mostly I want to discuss the ones men tell, because it goes hand and hand with the game. In this lesson, portions may be difficult to understand, so please follow closely. I won't turn the tables this time, because as a matter of fact, I'm quite fond of lies for a lot of reasons. It's a cat and mouse game of strategy I love to play. It excites and keeps me on my toes. It keeps my skills honed to perfection and sends chills up my spine with anticipation of victory… *and I always win!*

A word of caution when playing. As with most games you play with men, some are sore losers and don't take kindly if you happen to be the victor, so don't gloat or doddle. Collect your gains, and move on quickly! As I said, I'm not going to turn the tables on our counterpart, because I have something else in mind*. However, I will put a LARGE pretty lace tablecloth on this one…they're gonna *need* it!

Ducking, and dodging slipping and sliding*. Face it baby, for no apparent rhyme or reason, men lie. The things women say when men lie. "I saw you with my own eyes, I *saw* you. I know you're lying, 'cause your lips are moving!" Things men say to women when they lie. "Are you going to believe me or your lying eyes? Please listen baby, honest, she meant nothing to me. I love **you**."

Sound familiar? Yes, that's what they say, and have been getting away with it for eons. We have been trying to stay ahead of the lies men tell. Ladies we are spinning our wheels, fighting a needless battle that cannot be won. Women, we have got to stop thinking and repeating to other women, *you've got to get in, where you fit in.* I've heard this cliché way too many times, and frankly I've had my fill. Another male bullshit motto to excuse that fact he steps on the backs of others in order to achieve his greatness. Carve your *own* niche instead of waiting for one to be created for you. Use your whit and God given feminine wiles* to achieve your own greatness by building a better mouse trap. You *know* a lie is lie when you hear it! You don't have to go into a bag of tricks or transform yourselves into detectives like Sherlock Holmes or Colombo. Stop sugarcoating, making excuses, rationalizing, holding it up to the mirror at a different angle, trying to make it something it's not. When I smell the intoxicating aroma of Southern fried chicken wafting from the kitchen, I don't think clothes are being bleached in the sink! Or when a man passionately kisses me on my neck, I don't think he's attempting to use me as his next meal*! Be cognizant of *all* your senses*. Read* them, so you'll know when someone is lying to you*. Men lie. It's not worth wasting your time or losing any sleep over it. Woman up. It is what it is, and I'm going to call it exactly what it is, and not sugar coat it. A spade is a spade, fat meat is greasy*, and a lie is a fuckin' lie!!!! Got it? Moving on!

We are going to cover a lot of topics, and so far, I hope you are getting what you need from this. As I said earlier, I don't want to change the man, I just want to understand him. To me, he is God's Gift and want to know, if anything, I can do to make us to be more harmonious. We say its them, they say its us, back and forth, forth and back. We have got to stop pointing the finger and figure out how to make this work. I'm tired of being passed over because I have a pair of ovaries and he has a pair of nuts. I have found one thing to be true. The problem with most females, we try and fail when we compete with males on *their* level*. STOP THAT! They don't like it, and will go into battle mode*.

I'm sorry, I know this is not what you want to hear but it's the truth. I am going to be, if nothing else, brutally honest. I repeat, they will ALWAYS win if you try to compete with them on *their* level. Now that I've made you angry, you're sucking your teeth, and now, you calling me out of my name saying, I don't know what I'm talking about, just calm the hell down. That's the reason men call us bitch. Too emotional*! We asked to be lied to by men by asking the *wrong* questions. "Does this dress make me look fat? Where is this relationship going? Do you *really* love me? Did you fuck my best friend?"

You're an intelligent woman, you know your mate, you *know* the answer before you even ask it! The question you *should* be asking is do I know **me**? Ladies, stop over thinking the *problem*, work on a *solution*, and be **done** with it. Men are not that hard to figure out, we've established that! SEX is always on their brain. One of their secrets to know. **T F F***. Moving on!

They can care less if that damn dress makes you as you so coyly asked makes you look fat. You like it, wear. If not, wear something else. Stop stressing, eat less, do some light weight exercising, drop the pounds. *Done!*

Your relationship? Are you keeping him pleased and fucking him on the regular? Is he where you can put your hands on him at any given time of the day? I've got news for you queen, this *is* your relationship. Don't like it? Change it. There are three ways to do this, by still keeping your sense of worth and exude power in the process. *Tempt. Flatter. Feed**. Add some spice to your love making, remember he loves to play *all* games. Tempt him by learning and doing new sexual positions. This is no time to be a prude, this is *your* mate. If you don't satisfy his lusts, someone else will... longer. Flatter his ego with roll play* reversal. Pretend he's the big strong landlord coming to collect the rent. You, as the helpless tenant say, "Oh my stars, I've no money to pay, only this", exposing your bush. Then, faster than you can say, lickity-split, turn the tables on him. Feed him. Make him the kitty, and you the saucer of honey milk. If you're an alpha personality(or have a secret desire to become one) get a whip! Dominate, tie him up, make him your love slave for the evening. Of course, costumes are optional you sexy beast. *Done!*

So far as him really loving you, do you really love him? If not, maybe its time to take a good hard look at **you** and ask is this what I want for my life. Make a decision one way or another. There's nothing worse than living an unfulfilled life. *Done!*

A word about the female who calls herself your "best friend" once she betrays you. Drop the word *best,* drop the word *friend.* Matter of fact, drop her immediately! **No** form of apology from her can rectify this type of betrayal. She is dangerous to you, and to your well being. This toxic ameba bitch has proved she is not to be trusted, and if she fucked your man, she WILL fuck you, in other ways. What's the old saying, fool me once, shame on me, twice I'll ripe your heart out with a filthy spoon or some shit like that. Sigh, maybe it's just me. But seriously, never give someone the opportunity to betray you…*twice. Done and Done!*

Get a grip! You have Empires to conquer and Kingdoms to run. Woman the fuck up! I want you to stop frivolously wasting time, energy, and running around like headless chickens not knowing what to do. Many questions, both sides have them, both side feel their side is correct. Men say that women are the problem, women know men are. I know this can be a tough pill to swallow but, once and for all, from this time on, and moving forward, like it or not, *know* this. With men, sex is always on their mind, and men lie.

Something is either right, or its wrong. Simple enough right? Seems easy huh? Well, not really. With Mr. King of the jungle, it's nor black or white and can be tricky when dealing with our counterparts. Women can be as right as rain, with all your ducks in a row, see and *know* the sun rises in the East. Women can know, left from right, up from down and know that fat meat is greasy. Sadly, sometimes with men, you can win *and* lose* at the same time.

Part of the problem is ALL men think ALL women are the same and vice versa. Now, I know this is all too confusing for a novice, and it sounds like I'm going down a dark road into the abyss, but don't worry, you *know* I will clarify. I have something else in mind for the good ol' boys! Since I am a woman, I can only speak as one, therefore, can only offer up the difference from my point of view. Men, you are free to offer up your version at any time, when you're finished fighting useless battles that you start, measuring your dicks, fucking our friends, pissing on trees, setting imaginary boundaries, and playing with your planes.

MEET KANG BITCH!

Pardon me please, before I go any further, I ask for your indulgence for a few moments and allow me I to introduce myself to you. As you know, men and women have called me bitch for ages, and if you're going to force me to wear that title, so be it. There's nothing I can do to make you change your way of thinking. I will however make one small change. If and when you feel the need to refer to me in this manner again, I will now be known as…….. _**KANG BITCH!**_

Unbeknownst to you, I was not only being your Administrative Assistant, I was listening, watching, taking notes, and paying attention. Reading you*. I learned as a child to play games*, I love games. I'm _good_ at it. I've noticed you like games too. All games. Indoor games, outdoor games whether you participate or not. For me, poker is my game. I like poker because of its intensity. I've watched your every move very closely. Looking for the _tell_. In the poker arena, a tell is a vernacular term meaning a body movement. It's a clue as to what cards they are holding. Like wiping a brow, sweating, nervousness or shifting in the chair etc. It's an Achilles heel. A weakness. Everyone has a tell. I always observe my opponents. I size them up as I enter the room.

I have been educated at a school that is highly touted for it's illustrious and distinguished graduates. **KANG BITCH! _University_**. Lessons learned, accomplished, good, bad, or indifferent have brought me to this place in time. I *am* **KANG BITCH!** Large and in charge, big baller, shot caller! I say what I mean, and mean what I say. I didn't start the fire, but I **am** the flame. Beware! Cross me, you'll get burned! I'm the one your mothers warned you about. I can turn your dreams to nightmares and back again by my strength where once I was weak. It is you that cause this affect for me to hit the ground running in order to succeed.

You will know me because I am different from any of your regular ordinary run of the mill, garden variety, back alley, hood rat, street bitch. I am a witty complicated mix. I am strong, resourceful, humble, and independent, but most of all, I am determined to *win*. I will not utilize the dog eat dog tactics set by you in order to succeed, but I will use every tool in my arsenal to achieve and surpass the same heights as you. My interpersonal skills will thrust me forward, as I've learned a strong business sense and the "art of the deal" at your feet. You may view me as a threat to society, but I will *only* be one if you make me one. Remember, you were my teacher, I learned from watching you. I am impeccably dressed and coiffed, well manicured, and I am a highly intelligent professional woman, who will verbally go toe to toe with *any* man. I will corner you miserably and have you babbling incoherently, then leave you to wonder, what just happened to me? I do not cry, I do not stutter, I do not pout. I am eloquent and I am not intimidated by any man. **I intimidate!** Unlike you, my strength and confidence does not make me cold and unapproachable.

Make no mistake, I am *all* woman. Full bosoms, rounded hips that sway and look like someone from your most wildest erotic dreams, smelling like a sultry night drenched in apple blossoms. My honeycomb tinted skin, and red lips are at the ready to read ones with the misfortune to displease me. Fire red nails honed to tap when we are not amused, or to verbally scratch your eyes out if you speak unkindly. Then you'll say, "Now there's a **KANG BITCH!**" I'm not here to be your equal, but to be your *match.* And match you I will. I am very cognizant there's a game going on, and well aware of the rules on how to play. I may not win every battle, but blow for blow, I can and will defend my title. I came to ***win.*** I do not require, nor solicit your respect. I *demand* it. I am the result of your efforts. ***This*** is what happens when I am organized. **I *AM* KANG BITCH!**

As a woman, you are more detailed oriented*, therefore already **own** the key to success! I've learned there's a price that comes with winning and competing with men. The question is are you willing to pay the price? It's a high one!

Men have the upper hand because God Deemed it So. If you are a believer, man was the first human, therefore woman will always be second. Remember, being second doesn't mean second best, it only *means* second. I am the second child my parents had, but it doesn't mean I am second best. It only means my parents didn't have anymore children. Second can also mean new and improved. To the in the know, top of their game, women in advertising and marketing world that's a good thing, because they are smart. They know what works best with a woman's body.

Harsh additives, or pretty packaging is not the answer to improving a product. But to men…nnnnot so much.

You've probably seen the commercials stating, try this new bath crystals* its great! A few months later, that same commercial will come out advertising the *same* product, but now, with new additives and possibly new packaging, but now its "NEW and IMPROVED!*" Now its better more compact or more economical stronger or softer safer and cheaper than before. What the fuck!?! I just bought a shit load of your product took a bath in it. And **now** you're telling me it's new & improved because *possibly* it was not safe before? I don't care if I could get it for a cheaper price, or it's more compact or if tress in Sherwood Forest had to be chopped down, or you had to kill Bambi's mama to make it. I've got a scorching rash from sitting my coochie in this crap and it aint safe? What the hell am I suppose to do now? Next thing you know a class action law suit are in the works, lawyers are called in, monies paid to damaged consumers. Wheeling, dealing, maneuvering around the issues ducking and dodging, slipping and sliding, are you going to believe me or your lying eyes! Pictures shown of *your* offended area, insensitive questions asked about your extra marital sexual habits, numerous partners and positions. They use any and everything to discredit you to build a stronger case for *them*. In front of God and everyone, promiscuity was once was entered into question. You're stripped down, held up naked to the world to prove their case. They want to drive home the point, the next female will get the same treatment if they come up against them. They love flexing their muscles, beating their chests like King Kong and howling like mad dogs! They do not care.

You think, protect, protect, protect but going into protect mode could cost you to lose your case even if you win! Even if the plaintiffs say they lost, their lawyers would say we *won*. Yes **win**, even if they **lose**. Scratching your head, trying to make some sense of this? Wait a minute, you said, I *won* right? Yes. They were wrong, and yet I *lost*? Yes. And, I was *right*, and *won*? Yes. How could that be? Simple queen, more of that black white, up down, right left shit that's how! You won, but are left in the ashes licking your wounds from all the humiliation you had to endure. Now, your case is public record*, open to any snoop with curiosity issues to peruse all the sordid details at will. Win and lose at the same time. Do you *still* think you've won?

You have just learned first hand, now bear witness to the lies, how ruthless this man can be when protecting his own. Men will gather the wagons in a circle and go into battle mode against you. They have been doing this since the beginning of time. This is what they are good at *battle.* Men are willing to die for this! Are you? No? I don't blame you… neither am I. Put on your pretty red drawls queen! This is what I mean by competing with them on *their* level, you won't win. Red *must* be worn on the body in some form or fashion at all times when you leave your diva ass out the house to face the world. By that, I mean on some part of your body, red should be, but you must also be confident aggressive willing to fight for what's yours. I won't promise every battle fought will be won, but I will give you the tools so you won't loose miserably. READ* your opponent. Look at him/her. Study them closely. Can you take them on? Yes. You can take on anybody! Look at their body language and face*. Be confident, be poise, be self assured. If they are at ease with you, and keep constant eye contact, you can take them on! If they are ill at ease with you, fidgety, don't keep eye contact, shuffling papers, what have you, they are unsure of themselves and not aggressive, you can take them on! If they are a multi-millionaire, you can take them on! Do you see where I'm going with this? Say it for me Boo. A **KANG BITCH!** can take on *anybody*. You damn straight!

CHAPTER FOUR

THE LIBRARY IS OPEN
READ WITH RED!

Having a good time so far? Good. If you haven't already, incorporate red into your wardrobe. For my Alpha personalities, polish nails and toes a bright fire engine or tomato red. Blaze it! Flaunt it! Own it! Find the most alluring red lipstick for beautiful pouty lips. Buy an airy flouncy to the knees bright red skirt that adds just a touch of booty bounce because queen you've got a lot to say and you want to look glamorous walking away! To my oh so demure types, if you're not yet bold enough to wear it all over, or want to ease into it that's fine too. Don't be afraid of red, it's a neutral color like black or white it goes with *everything*. Join in my sideliners. Sport some red stud earrings or a red stone ring. How 'bout a colorful red scarf in your hair, wrap it onto your purse, use as a belt. Or, wear some bright red sexy panty and matching bra no one has to know…but *you'll* know. It'll be you're little secret. A woman feels power when she's holding a secret. I want you to *feel* sexy. The whole point is for **all** of you to *feel* the power of red. Interchange, mix it up, don't be timid, or sit back and watch shit happen, just *do* it dammit! You'll thank me later queen.

EYES. Folklore has stated are the windows to the soul. The eyes play a huge part when speaking to people we meet. It shows if we are engaged completely in the conversation or if something else has caught our attention. It is very important when meeting with MONEY that you keep and hold* the attention by looking at MONEY directly in the eye. This shows you are interested in what MONEY is saying even if MONEY is boring the shit out you. MONEY is feeding you. MONEY is putting a roof over your head. MONEY has the potential to put an even larger roof over your head. Are you fucking paying attention? Sometimes it's hard, but try to get plenty of rest if you're going to meet with MONEY. Bright, pretty, happy eyes are easy to talk to. Bloodshot, sleepy, crusty eyes gets you no conversation at all! Any drug store brand or name brand eye clarifiers are fine, but don't use too often as it has the tendency to irritate.

FACE. While at the drug store, buy a buff puff, cocoa butter lotion and Dove or Caress soap. Every night *gently* scrub face, neck and décolletage area with soap and warm water. Pat dry. Moisturize with cocoa butter lotion paying close attention around the eyes. Do not put anything else on your face before going to bed. Most women slather on product after product wondering why their face has lost its glow, looks pale or has acne. The body replenishes itself at night automatically. Don't interfere with this normal process.

HAIR. Can't achieve it, weave it! Can't grow it, sew it! There's absolutely nothing wrong with improving upon, or adding human hair extensions or a wig because fashion dictates it, medical reasons requires it or you just simply want to update your do…as long as it *looks* natural.

Remember: *Image is everything!*

Find a color, length, texture that matches your own. For the record, save the Sexy Blond Bombshell or Purple Passion Enchantress and Elvira lookalike for *roll play* you sexy beast! Before you commit to something as drastic as a cut, visit your local wig shop and try on a few wigs in the style you have in mind. Ooooo! There's a cute lace front wig! Does it tickle your fancy? Try it on gurrl. Do you Boo! **Do *you.*** Maybe you are a queen who can't stand anything on their head, or have hair to throw back in a ponytail if needed. Be it straight or curly, short and sassy, or wash and wear, the air dries my hair, or my hair looks best doing its own thing, lock it, braids, au natural, perm it, dye it, or touch up that kitchen. Whatever your preference, keep it clean. I'm not going to tell you what to do with your hair because us girls know what works best for *our* hair. All I'm going to say is KEEP IT CLEAN! KEEP IT CONDITIONED! KEEP IT STYLED!

VITAMINS. *My dear queen. Before following any of these suggestions, or you are taking prescriptive medications, please check with your doctor first.*

Get a female gynecologist. She can offer help and will be more sympathetic to your needs. Every woman should take a multi-vitamin. Also, include a fish oil/flaxseed supplement to keep your heart healthy. I love drinking caffeine free green or black tea. It is very refreshing, quenches thirst, and good for you.

Okay my Princess. Let's take a break. Relax. *Breath.*

A love letter to the men.

I am the best thing that ever happened to you and you are my world. I love and adore you. I am a part of you, and you are a part of me. I am strong. I am unique. I am a powerful. I am only second by chance, not by choice, which makes me strong, but not the weaker sex. I am capable of tremendous feats, and can accomplish all I set in motion.

For generations, I am the first teacher of all generations.
In excoriating pain, from me you came. Cradled in my arms, you drew my life giving fluid to nourish your body. I was the first to teach you love, compassion and understanding. From my voice you learn to speak. Vowel by vowel, syllable by syllable, until you were able to speak coherently. My heart leaped when you said your first word!
Under my watchful eye, you crawled. My hand guides the way for your first adventurous step, then walk, then stand. There's a reason why you no longer fall on your face, I taught you to tie your shoe laces. Do you remember baby? Make two rabbit ears, and tie a bow. No more "accidents" because I was the one who potty trained you. On a stormy night, I was your protector from monsters under the bed, when it was to my arms you ran. And a kiss or two for boo-boos.

I comforted you through good and bad times. When they rained on your parade, I was your umbrella. There to offer a soothing touch, an understanding heart, when a first crush goes awry. I rubbed your head, gave you a cookie and said everything is going to be alright. Through my wise tutelage, you learned how to treat a lady, act like a gentleman and have good manners. The pain was endured out of love for you, but all these things I have done, I will gladly continue to do so much more, because it is my nature. *You,* are the best thing that ever happened to me. I am strong. I am unique. I am powerful. I am only second by chance, not by choice.

I am your mother, your sister, your daughter, your wife, your grandmother, your cousin, your friend. I am *all* the women in your life.

I've loved. I've taught. I've comforted. I've protected. From my voice you learn. How can you *still* call me bitch?

Now, let's resume…

Speech. In the words of Jaime Fox's character "Ugly Wanda" from In Living Color, "I got chuu!" In this portion of our lessons, you'll learn if nothing else, how to talk to a man. Do you know there's a difference when speaking to a man as apposed to speaking to a woman? You didn't? Well suga, it's true!

We all need some me time to just let loose and let off some steam and be ourselves. Let your hair down, hell take it off let it breath! In one's homes when speaking with your gurrls, you're at ease. Throwing caution to the wind, you are not aware of you're your language. Just about anything falls out of your mouth including food, without any hesitation or fear of repercussions. Have a few more lemon drop martinis, or top self golden margaritas on the rocks rimmed with salt or sugar, fully loaded nachos and the hotter the better hot wings and its party over here! You are loud, boisterous, arms flaying about slapping knees and each other on the arm leg back etc.. Paying little or no attention to how you are sitting or if anything is being exposed. Weather a boob happens to slip out, we don't care! We feel comfortable around our gurrls. Lick your fingers, smack your lips. After all, it's our gurrls! They understand as it should be. They wouldn't be your gurrls if they didn't! And if after one too many cocktails, we should happen to need a ride home or a designated driver*, not to worry, I'm yo gurrl, I got chuu! But, that is the *only* time you should and can be yourself, BEHIND CLOSED DOORS. In the sanctity of one's home! When in the presence of a man, you MUST, WILL, and ALWAYS act differently. You say, "I feel comfortable around men. Why do I have to put on any these airs for them?"!@^%$!#@!!@!!! I am really trying to refrain from cursing so much, but if you ask one more asinine question, you will get the full force of my wrath. Just listen, and DO!

A 'Death Stare'. To look fixedly at someone with so much hate in hopes that their face melts, explodes or caves in with extreme discomfort and pain. To get your **POINT** across to a man/client you must have a death stare type of a look once you engage him in conversation. This will keep and hold his attention.

Do not smile. Do not tilt your head to either side.

I implore you to follow the last instruction verbatim when expressing your point. I've had the misfortune of noticing this when a woman is deeply engaged in conversation with a man. She wonders why she is not getting through to him, because he is not taking her seriously. He thinks you're flirting! Tilt your head* from side to side is a flirtation move. You look like a school girl with a crush. You might as well kick the dirt and twirl your hair around your finger while talking to him. Why don't you just fix him an extra dry vodka martini have slippers at the ready Donna! Yes, I know it's a girl thing, slightly tossing your head back, running your hands through your hair, fluttering your eyes, licking your lips…I know *all* the tricks. If **you** don't, we'll cover that under flirting*. You are there to close a *deal*, not make a *meal!* Do not tilt* your head, keep your head still! To **TALK** to a man/client, follow the rule above…*except smile!*

In public, throwing caution to the wind, and not being mindful of your language is **forbidden.** Once you have become indoctrinated as a **KANG BITCH!**, the use of foul language, street slang, or even Ebonics is never ever tolerated inside the Realm. Make a trip to your local library if you don't have a computer to keep abreast of the latest "catch phrases" uses, meanings, and jargon, of the corporate world. While there, or online, brush up on the English language *and* diction.

Chiiill aint nuttin lik trin'n' ta tawk ta sumbydee dat dunt 'stan wha 'chu saa'n!

Your first meet with your client is an important one, so make sure you are fully prepared. The night before, lay out your clothes paying special attention that there's no stains, or needs repairing. Rehearse a few times your game plan as if it were a play and you're the Star! This will give you confidence when you finally make you entrance. If you're not sure how to say a word, in a mirror, carefully enunciate each syllable out loud. Then say the word twice to yourself to remember it. Good luck queen, you got this!

CLIENT FIRST MEET

Remember, you are the walking billboard advertisement for your business. That means you must be on point, open for business, ready to hit the ground running once you walk you're your fabulous diva ass out the front door! Having the knowledge on how to promote yourself is a given, but the art of knowing how to "dress" your billboard is most important of all. It's very simple, men are visual creatures*, and there are only *three* factors to consider when choosing an outfit for your first meet.

WEATHER. TIME OF DAY. LOCATION.

The weather will dictate how you should dress for the day or evening of your first meet. Make sure to check the local news for any unforeseen weather changes in case you need to add a jacket, an umbrella or boots to your glorious ensemble. Maybe you need to change your whole outfit! You be the judge.

Pardon me ladies, there's something I must tell you. I know I'm about to break your little heart, and for that I apologize. I am here to shake up your life, change your way of thinking, acting, and looking. I'm going to turn your world upside down, inside out, basically make it better so you can stop merely functioning in this man's world, and to become a more active intricate part in the advancement for a knowledgeable women to succeed. With that said, for your first meet, no jeans. Quit whining, woman up, get over it! You want the time to be convenient for your client, but for you also, so a compromise is in order, but always in his favor. Remember, time is money, and you will *always* make time for *his* money. Always be dressed professionally. What if the meet is a beach setting? I **know** you're not going to wear them fuckin' flip flops!!!

The meet is scheduled by him, who pays? YOU! Unless otherwise specified. Anytime *you* ask, schedule, generate, call for, text, request a meet with a prospective client, the tab is always on you Boo. He has the money, you want the money. Ever heard of you have to spend make to make money? Well, this is a prime example of that, so choose a place a place that is well within your means, with a bar and convenient for both you and your client to drive. MapQuest directions if needed.

FOOD/EATING/ALCOHOL

If your client wants to meet at a restaurant, coffee shop are anything that involves eating, be at your best by following these simple procedures. Eat a some crackers or half a sandwich with a large glass of milk or fruit juice *before* your meet to curb your appetite. Remember you are there for business, *not* to eat. **Pay attention.** Don't be disrespectful by ordering an elaborate main courses like prime rib, Maine lobster, pheasant under glass, or oysters Rockefeller. Save that for when you close the deal! Keep it light, but substantial. He is watching your every move, even what you order.

Example: He. A medium rare steak, baked potato with "the works", Jack on the rocks. You. House salad, no croutons, dressing on the side, iced tea, sweet and low, lemon wedge, which **SKA-REAMS** bitch on a diet! Have you lost your damn mind?!? He's not going to trust some anorexic, salad eating, sweet and low sprinkling, tea drinking, carb watching, water weight retaining, calorie counting, lemon squeezing hussy with any new ideas! If you can't control your eating habits, why the *hell* should he trust you to control his business ventures? Count calories, each finger, your loud ticking biological clock, sheep or whatever on your own fuckin' time! This is a part of the business *Game!* Pay attention to what he ordered. He's a lean mean fighting machine! This man works out daily. How else can he afford to eat and drink this way? This man is your true masterful business *Game* player and he came to play. While you still had sleep in your eyes this morning, he was calculating how he was going to eat you for lunch! He's bulking up to win and your salad eating ass is about to get left in the dirt losing miserably and dying from hunger. He is open for business, and out on the prowl. You'd better pay attention, he's on the hunt….for you! Don't be his prey.

He's a gamer, but he's also a gentleman, so he'll let you order first. If you're unsure as to what to order, there's a way to get around this say, "Everything looks so good, what would *you* suggest?" Now this ploy can be tricky, because it can almost be detected as being indecisive on your part, but smile, baby smile. You might throw him off a bit. This is killing two birds with one stone. One, you are getting out of a sticky situation because you don't know what to order. Two, you are letting him know how much you value his opinion, and trust me, he *is* taking notice. If still in doubt, order the same or something similar. Moving on!

When the food arrives, make good use of *both* knife and fork. Cut food into even smaller pieces than you are use to before putting into your mouth. After cutting your food, place knife across plate at top, not at the side of the plate. You will be speaking quite a bit and don't want food flying out of your mouth in the process. Pay attention to him *not* your food. Speak in short direct sentences. Keep to the point and do not stray from your topic of conversation. Women have a tendency to ramble on and repeat. If you do that, you'll notice when you lose him, he will get that far away glassy eyed stare. It's is how a man looks like when he's cornered. You know the look, *you've seen it.*

Scenario. "Honey, I know mom is a handful and you don't get along with her, but her house is being fumigated, so she's staying with us for a few weeks". *That look.* Or, "I thought you said you were at Fred's house yesterday. I saw him today and he said he hasn't seen you all week!" *That look.* Or, you go to the car wash, let the seat back for cleaning and find a pair of size three crouch less panties…they're not yours. You present them to him. Can you see his face? Or, you, in his face, hands on hips, waving around the recent phone bill as evidence screaming like a banshee and waiting for an instant reply to your question saying, **"WHAT IN THE FUCK IS 1-800-DIAL-A-HOE?!?"** Yup. *That* look!

End Scenario

To my head strong Alpha personalities. Try not to take *full* charge of this meet. Let him hold the chair for you and open the door. Wait until he finishes when he is speaking and don't out talk him. Or be the "The Ice Queen", someone who is hard to get along with, unapproachable, or worse, a *real* bitch. Be flexible, be endearing, be agreeable, until you get your foot in the door, *then* you can be big baller shot caller **KANG BITCH!** We can always castrate him later in the Tower if he doesn't meet our demands…Just kidding!

To my demure wallflower, and passive sideliner pumpkins. You *can* do this. Take a deep cleansing breath and release it. Jump in there with both feet. Woman up! You have a mouth, use your words! Be precise. Be direct. Keep eye contact. But remember, this is *his* business meet and you must maintain a level of professionalism or you will not be taken seriously. Think of yourself/company as an opportunity he cannot afford to let slip through his fingers. You *can* do this!

Again, careful not to flirt, accidently or otherwise. This is not the time to play the damsel in distress, flip or twist your hair, can you open this bottle because I might chip a nail, cut my steak, swoon and have the vapors because it's much too hot for your fragile delicate body. Allegedly, in Hollywood the "Casting Couch" was infamous. There's no need for a casting couch in the Realm*. You don't want to be known in the corporate world as "The Tart", sleeping your way to the top, legs open for every Tom, Dick, or Harry. *If* the client insists on paying, make sure he pays for the *food* not the *mood*!

Before the meal/coffee is over, excuse yourself to the ladies room to make necessary repairs, hair, makeup but don't take too long primping. Remember his short attention span? *Keep in mind the topic on hands.* When you return to the table, make sure your client has your portfolio, business card, proposal, and any other necessary paperwork in a nice professional binder. **IMAGE IS EVERYTHING!** Leave any uneaten food behind. I don't care how hungry or broke you are, or how delicious the food was, under **no** circumstance are you to take a doggy bag. Asking for a doggy bag is highly offensive especially if you did not pay for the food. If your client insists you take a doggy bag, and he doesn't. **DO NOT** take the food. Make up an excuse about not going directly home, or you have another appointment and it might spoil. It's a power ploy and he's playing you. Let him know by your actions you not only came to play, and you came to win! Keep your guard up. Remember what's always on their mind? Give a femininely warm smile and a firm hand shake.

Your Image. Protect it as if it were a newborn child. The way a person sees us if of great concern and no where else does this matters most than in the field of media. How many times have we heard gossip columnists say unkind things about our favorite stars that changed your outlook of them. This star is sleeping with another's husband or wife can change your view of them in a New York minute. Or if suddenly an attractive single hunk is now off the market, it rips you to your core that he now has a wifey poo, or you found out they are gay. As if you had a chance in hell either way! **Image.** It's the way we are *seen*, not necessarily the way we *are*.

CHAPTER FIVE

WOMAN LADY GIRL FEMALE

My Creole mother, God rest her soul, once said, "Females are some back biting, talking behind your back, eye rolling, sleeping with men that's not theirs low down so on so's chérie. Not giving any thought to the hurt feelings of other women." While playing with my dolls at her feet, I remember one particular hot afternoon while she was hanging laundry on the line, I over heard her say to one of her friends over the backyard fence. She said, "Females are so dirty chérie, they won't even tell you if you're slip is hangin' no!" I thought then, that's sad, and then later when I was older, that's cruel! They're like a bunch of crabs in a barrel*. As soon as one makes it to the top, the others pull him down.

She said he said, I saw your man coming out the motel with some bitch last night bullshit, that cuts deeper than any knife. If a woman has a nice house, we say she's living above her means. Maybe she has on a stunning designer outfit or displaying fine to die for jewelry, we say arrogantly, must be nice! Whispers, pointing, slow head turning, catty remarks and looking at you up and down when you enter the room as if you've stepped in and smell like shit! As I got older, I thought a lot about things my mother taught me, but mostly I'm paying closer attention to what *words* she used.

Going back in my memory, the event of my mother is clear as a bell on that hot afternoon when she was talking to her girlfriend over the back fence. Funny how that happens. I can remember something that happened over…ahem, a while ago, but I can't remember what I had for breakfast last Friday! She used the word *females* not women, girls, or even ladies. Makes me think. Words. Simple words. Hard words Easy words. All words. I love them. I like to decipher them. I like to pick them apart, like I do men. Just like men calling us bitch, you can't change these females way of thinking…but excuse me while I whip out my pretty little lace tablecloth!

Uppers. Downers. Maryjane. Coke. Ecstasy. LSD. Orange Sunshine. Purple Haze. Don't get scared, it's not what you think. You are so silly…but I like your style! In this application, I would like to think of our gender as a DRUG. After all, women are intoxicating and I feel this is a playful way to show it. There are two definitions. The *World's Definition.* The way the world defines or sees you without fully understanding, and the *Actual Truth.* The story told by **You**, when understanding is fully explained or achieved. We've all been scared in one way or another. We all must take a good hard look at our lives, stop pointing fingers and make necessary changes. Isn't the objective to learn from mistakes made? There's an old saying that goes, …"Money knows money, game knows game, and every preacher knows a pimp…" Unless you have walked in *their* shoes, there's no way you can offer an opinion, or make a judgment call on what's going on in *their* life. It's a shame we can't go around with little note pads in hand explaining the situations in our lives. Hopefully, this will make you take pause before making any rash decisions about someone you don't know if you don't have **all** the facts. There are four categories. WOMAN. LADY. GIRL. FEMALE. At the end, *Further Definition* which is self explanatory.

World's Definition.

Woman. Pure version. Only one lover. Has been off the porch, but never off the block if you catch my drift. She's a one man's woman. Poised, and well dressed, she is the one a man wants in his home and at his side. Introduce to the parents, bear and rear his children, clean his house, cook his meals. Model of society. The scars she carries are on the inside. No freak here.

Sexual Position and Frequency: Missionary position only. 1 or 2 times a week.

Lady. Been stepped on. Now, she *has* been off the block, but managed to find her way back without stirring up any rumors. Has scars, but covers them well with cosmetics plus, she's learned a thing or two. Appropriate for social occasions and gatherings, excellent conversationalist, will procreate for a price, cook sometimes. Arm candy. Be sure you get a get prenuptial with her. Potential freak…but not with you.

Sexual Position and Frequency: Missionary. Maybe if you beg, her on top. 2 to 3 times a week as long as if doesn't interfere with her hair, nails, spa day, and Pilates.

Girl. Mixed bag. Been off the block, around the corner, down the street, across the alley and stoned most of the time. Young. Cute. Bouncy. Energetic. *Always* chewing gum, or sucking on her fingers. Says she has a mouth fetish. Not yet fully housebroken, no social function but she to loves to go 'clubbin' and gettin' wasted dude. A little wet behind the ears but tolerable, because she's cute and bouncy. Has tendency to call you daddy. She has scars but covers them with tattoos. Super duper freak. Hummm…Two words. Buy condoms!

Sexual Position and Frequency: Heeey, like let's party man!

Female. Seeds. Stems. Rocks. Dirt etc. Was driven off the block and out the neighborhood by good decent God fearing Christians. Went down the block, around the corner, across the alley. Got on a bus, moved to another state. Came back home scared by circumstance….*three times.* Several children by numerous men. Will screw *any* man…for a price. Bottom of the barrel. Slut. Whore. Tramp.

Sexual Position and Frequency: Are you serious? You still wanna fuck this bitch!?!

WOMAN. LADY. GIRL. FEMALE. We can look at each one of them, woman, lady, girl, female and find fault when in actuality it could be one of your friends, or a loved one, or maybe….

Actual Truth.

The <u>WOMAN</u> who is pure is what we all start out as once she leaves the comfort and security of her parent's home. Whether we marry or find our own little slice of heaven in a new loft or apartment, we have high expectations and all is **brand new**. The purchase of furnishings, drapes, even buying a waste paper basket is a new shopping adventure. So many new decisions. Maybe I'll put the couch here, and a throw rug there. A plant would look nice in that corner! Sex is the furthest from your mind. Well, I don't think he cares *that* much about it. I was a virgin when we met, besides, he knows I don't know too much about sex, but I'll try and hope I please him. Well, it **does** mean a lot to him and try as you may, you fail. Hearing the words "Keep your dress down and your panties up" resonate in your ears as you try to please your man and satisfy his lurid(to you)sexual needs. You are left alone in the world with kids to wonder what did I do wrong, as he moves on to one more experienced and less timid.

The <u>LADY</u> who has learned a thing or two, realizes now that it's all about **me.** She's willing to submit to his needs as long as he submit to hers…first. For my adult life I've had a husband and children making constant demands, being the chef, chauffer and bottle washer, tending boo-boos, bookkeeping, shopping, refereeing sibyl rivalry, are just some of the jobs of being a wife and mom…. all for free! I'm at the end of my tether. I'm not about to get my well manicured nails chipped doing dishes or bowing down to pick up your dirty drawls off the floor without you dangling a diamond bracelet. You went into our little arrangement with your eyes wide open, now you want to back out! I told you up front I didn't want anymore children, and you were fine with that. *We* had an **agreement**, I look good, you take care of everything else. I'll cook, but *I do not clean.* I'm holding up my end of the bargain, I'm the lady of the house, not the maid! Then you're left to wonder what went wrong, when he moves on to one who is not so high maintenance.

The <u>GIRL.</u> Ahhh to be a girl again. This was the point in my life where my mother took pity on me and felt I was due a much needed break. She knew what I had been going through, a broken marriage and such, so she took the kids off my hands for the summer. I packed up their things and off to the grandparents they went. A kiss for each sweet cheek and a promise to see them next weekend and out the door I go. Yeah!

The early 70's was all about enjoying different cultures, sipping from the cup of kindness, sampling the earth's treasures, loving freely, peace, harmony and embracing your fellow man. It was a coming of age for Baby Boomers. Clubs, house parties a *free to be me* time**.** No cares or worries, come and go as you please, throw caution to the wind, fly by the seat of your pants, wind in your hair. Who cares what happens tomorrow, I'm living for today. I'm going to do all the things I was told not to. Talk loud and draw a crowd, curse like a drunken sailor, chew gum. Oh, I just learned how to pop it! Just like Denise Nicholas did in the movie *Let's do it again,* with Bill Cosby and Sidney Poitier, but it keeps sticking to my new dental work, so I have to keep dislodging it with my fingers! One older guy saw me doing this, so I decided to have a little fun with him by doing a little baby-talk saying, "I have a mouth fetish daddy." He started drooling like a baby! Men are such little boys. The mere mention of *possible* head gets 'em hard! Someone says, "Hey! Where's my fuckin' coke spoon? Oh, it's around my neck …found it!" Another yells, "Hey, let's go to Tijuana! ROAD TRIP!!!!" And we're all in. "Yo, Babe, another vodka stinger…Oooo you're cute…can I hit that?! You're a good kisser…what's your name again? Hey let's play strip poker!!!" You have loads of friends, you were having fun, and you thought he was too, yet he moves on to one who is not so *friendly.* Hey daddy, where ya going?!? Fuck yooou!! Let's party…Yo babe, another vod…Oooo, can I hit that?!?

The <u>FEMALE</u>. A dimpled good looking female has it's advantages…and disadvantages. It can get you in and out of trouble sporty! Being a single parent is rough, there's never enough money. "Gotta steal from Peter to pay Paul", as my mother, God rest her soul use to say. I go to work, come home, sleep, pay bills, cook, play with the kids, help with homework that's my days *and* nights. I've got two jobs with no help from their father, and it seems every time I run into a man, he thinks I'm an easy lay because I'm a single parent. Well, I'm not…I'm just lonely. I know what the touch of a man feels like and I miss it dearly. I have urges and needs and I have them often. Luckily, there's a teenager that lives next door who doesn't mind babysitting at a moments notice.

I drop off the kids next door and tuck them in for the night. I invite my male visitor to come sit in my parlor. I ask that he bring some bacon, eggs or a box of cereal and milk for my children's breakfast along with the drink and my cigarettes. He act as if I asked for a side of beef and all the fixings. Shit my kids gotta eat! I've got to look after their well being every chance I get! If I ask for a few dollars for gas or lunch money for work the next day, he act as if it was a pussy payment. TRUST, If he took me out to dinner, he would've spent *that* and **more** and still went home with blue balls! Thanks to that blabber mouth teenager, whom I tried to school on the ways of the world, on how to act like a lady because she's fuckin every little boy that comes in the house while her poor mother was at work, told everybody *all* my business and gets it wrong in the process. This is the same little ignorant slut that got 200 on her SAT's and *thought* she spelled her name right, told the whole neighborhood ***I'm*** hoeing. Now my kids are being teased because of me and we have to move. People pointing there finger and whispering. Saying nasty things about me my and kids behind my back. We love this neighborhood, they love their school. That's not fair! It's not true! That's alright, one monkey don't stop no show! I'm going to be a success one day. I'll show them. Gotdamn self righteous ass good for nothing back stabbing bastards!

Further definition.

Each character contributes in some way to a personality. WOMAN. All is *brand new*. It's is when we are at our most venerable*.

The somewhat virtuous woman wanted so much to set a good example for her children and be the "good wife". That is not possible when you have a mate that only understands he is the master of his domain. You and your needs comes second. Thank God we learned it doesn't stay that way!

LADY. A *verbal* agreement from him that is fair, though some may think she's selfish. The lady takes what she wants, but there's not a selfish bone in her body. She learns that in order to make it in this man's world, there must be a *written* agreement. Get it in writing, have it notarize, take a picture of it, commit it to memory, but dammit make sure he understands exactly *up front* what the conditions are. Of course he'll agree, a lot of men will, but then back out when things get tough or don't go their way. Like a two year old little boy, and an appendage to match, he throws tantrums, kicks and screams. Thinking and saying to yourself, "I've raised kids, I don't need this shit!" The best thing for you to do is leave. So you pack up your Dior and Gucci and do just that. Smooches! Wow! That was a learning experience!! Was the perfect wife, got screwed. Was once referred to as his *on call ice bitch*. Got screwed there too…and not in a good way.

GIRL. The cute misunderstood irrepressible party girl with her child-like ways and care free attitude. Her *free to be me* playful side, can sometimes by those who don't know her, be misconstrued as being wild or loose. How many times have we wished for a break from the norm to throw caution to the wind? I'm a responsible person, I've followed all the rules, but now I need a drink. ROAD TRIP!?! Well, we all know how **that** turned out. But you know what? I wouldn't have missed it for the world 'cause I had a great time!

FEMALE. She's tried it *all*, only to be left alone because she wanted to please her man. The focused strong willful female who takes care of **all** but no one to care for her…*yet*. She's not a bad person, not really. Well, let's say, she didn't start out that way, none of us did. *Circumstance* made her that way. The female, is the whole ball of wax. She is always in need…but aren't we all? Through it all, she manages to brush herself off and get back on her feet. I for one, admire and applaud a person like this because no matter what life throws her way, she stays strong, she stays focused, and keeps her eye on the prize.

Style. Grace*. You either have it or you don't. One can be taught, the other from good genes. Oh really? I feel they *both* can be acquired. Anyone can be taught to have style and grace with a little patience, a soft hand, and a tolerant heart. Personalities can become traits. Each One *Can* Teach One.

I *am* **KANG BITCH!**

EQUETTE

I would like to dedicate this section to my mother. I have been Blessed abundantly to have a wonderful patient woman in my life to raise and teach me the intricate ways on how to be a lady. Although shy with a protective upbringing, she was a very smart woman. She had the *know* how, to teach a headstrong willful child through play.

I love being a woman and all that it implies. Thanks to God and my parents, I had a great childhood. Playing assorted board games with my brother on a rainy day was fun…until I constantly won! So I turned my attention to dressing up. It was one of my favorite things to do as a child. My mother was a true girly-girl, so I had a vast array of wondrous colorful items to tickle any little girl's fancy when it was time to play.

While we were home alone one rainy Spring day, we had put aside some old clothes she was going to donate, and one box for my playtime. It was like Christmas for me as we separated them. Old clothes that smelled from the hint of moth balls and dust. Rummaging, sneezing and watching her face as she remembers when she held up a tattered old fur saying, "Your daddy gave me this", I pulled out long strings of pearls, oodles of sparkling clear diamonds, tons of my birth stone bright green emeralds, buckets of red rubies, heaps of deep blue sapphires, milky white opals and every gem imaginable. Oooooo!!! Of course they were all costume jewelry, but to me it was a pirate's treasure trove! High heel shoes galore. Mother loved high heel shoes, with stockings. You know the kind with the seams in the back? Wonder why they stop making those? *Very* sexy! Dresses, skirts, no pants…mother never wore pants, blouses, jackets, sweaters, gloves, felt hats with the pull down netting and her signature red lipstick. Quicker than you can bat an eye, I was set to play dress up.

One thing you should know, that as a child, I was very precise. There were certain foods I would not eat, my food couldn't be "touching" on my plate(I still don't like it) and my clothes were spray starched and not by using Argo because it irritated me and every game had a title. I know, I was a pain in the ass, but even then, I *knew* what I liked and what I wanted.

She would start dinner for the family and I would start my transformation from little girl to "Proper Lady" in my room. That's what my game was called. Proper Lady. Mother picked the title. Hummmm. I'd put on her dress, a string of pearls, rubies and diamonds, gloves, that tattered old fur, a jacket and mother's shoes, her felt hat lipstick, then stumble my way into the kitchen where she is still preparing dinner. Trying, in a very grown voice, I said, "How do I look chérie?"

I'd learned from my mother at a very young age how to **read** people not only by their words, but also by their body language. Using this strategy soon became second nature to me, as I remember her saying…

Watch me closely Baby. **Look** *at someone when you ask a question chérie. If you ask a* **direct** *question, they don't hesitate, and give you a* **direct** *answer, they are telling the truth. If they* **hesitate**, *they're lying. If they adjust themselves in any way, stall, or look around after hearing the question, they are* **still** *lying.*

She hesitated and smile.

"You look good."

Studying her face and feeling disappointed I asked, "What did I do wrong?" Thus begin our Proper Lady lessons. She turned the eyes under the pots on the stove on low, washed her hands, dried them on her crisp freshly ironed white apron and we sat down at the kitchen table.

A lady must be a lady at all times. Sit up straight with your back against the back of the chair. The proper way to cross your legs at the ankles, never across the knees where your thighs can be exposed. Hold your cup in hand and the saucer in the other, one must not leave the other when sipping. If drinking wine or cordial hold at stem. Do not slurp. Noise should never be heard when a lady is eating. No gum chewing. Ooops, I forgot. *Hands are to be kept away from your face crossed on lap and not on table. Napkin is placed on lap while at the table. If you must leave the table, excuse yourself from your guest, remove the napkin from your lap, dab the corners of your mouth to remove any excess food particles and place on side of plate never on back of chair or chair seat. A lady has a soft almost melodic voice. No foul language should be uttered from a lady's lips.* Fuck! I forgot that! Too many vodka stingers…and blow…and…

60

shit. Hey, I was on summer break don't judge, just read on! *You want a man to lean in when he speaks to you so make sure your fragrance isn't offensive or too strong. When purchasing a fragrance for yourself don't ask the counter girl. Take a few samples over to the men's fragrances counter, ask for a few of **his** suggestions then make your selection from that. Take your time applying makeup. Draw a cupid's bow when applying lipstick for nice even looking lips. Diamonds or pearls. Jacket or fur. One or the other, never together chérie.*

I remember telling my mother, boys are so disgusting. Smiling she said, you won't feel like that for long, they do grow up you know. I found out, boy did they ever! All kinds of boys and all cute! I was too young for car dates, but I could have porch dates. Not allowed to wear makeup yet, I was fascinated by it at an early age. Shopping with mother while buying her signature red lipstick, or going to the show on a Saturday afternoon. On this huge screen, I saw up close, stunning ladies with beautifully applied makeup and perfectly arched lips and eyebrows! "See that?" mother says pointing to the screen, then to her lips, tracing around them, "That's as a cupid's bow, men like that." I nod with wide eyed enthusiasm and amazement. I loved watching romantic old black and white movies with her. It was there I learned to be coy, and learned the true art on how to flirt!

FLIRTING

From Wikipedia, the free encyclopedia. **Flirting** or **coquetry** is a social and sometimes sexual activity involving verbal or written communication as well as <u>body language</u> by one person to another, suggesting an interest in a deeper relationship with the other person. In most cultures, it is socially disapproved for a person to make explicitly sexual advances, but indirect or suggestive advances (i.e., flirting) may at times be considered acceptable.

Presentation. How something looks and what catches the eye. I have driven ten miles out of my way to go to another store, simply because it was cleaner than the less expensive one. By the same token, I will bypass a handsome well tailored man, if has bad table manners. That's MY deal breaker! Men are visual creatures. Are you a pretty visual package? *Every* woman should know how to flirt. Once mastered, the art form known as flirting, can get you in and out of some delicious sexual and nonsexual situations! I want you to use your imagination to it's *fullest degree*, and be cognizant of *all your senses*. Use them, play with them, let them breath.

Sight. Hearing. Smell. Touch. Taste.

Now we will uncover some titillating and tantalizing pleasures! Ladies as stated, I have disclosed some of their well kept secrets. In this lesson, I will disclose some of *ours.*

Don't hold your breath, I won't tell *all*(smile). We want men to *think* that we've purchased that slinky little number for them but in actuality, it's a known fact, we women dress for each other. You see a cute guy/girl(I don't judge)and you want to get their attention. Hey, flirting is flirting! Want to turn heads when you enter the room, or when you're sitting down? Two words. **Diva Dress!** We are all beautiful women no matter what your size. Our society dictates that we be model size 2 or 3, and designers back them up by making clothing in this style. Well dammit, I'm NOT a size 2 or 3, nor do I wish to be. I am a full bodied, built for comfort not speed, well rounded hips, curvy, grown ass woman. I like *real* food. If you take me out to dinner and order me a salad, there had better be a magician joining us so he can feed it to the rabbit in his fuckin' hat! All I'm saying is you can still enjoy the same foods as always, just eat less or make a few small changes. Want a hamburger? Just take off the top bun. Order apple slices instead of fries or carry an apple and green tea or flavored water with you. Love fried chicken? Two piece with sides not three! Pizza? Sure. Only try more veggies and meatball instead of the fatty pepperoni and Italian sausage. Or, here's a novel idea. *Cook!* The thing is, not to become weight obsessed, but to be weight conscious. Buy clothing that accentuates your best sexy feminine features. We *all* have something we like about ourselves. Be it our hair, face, breast, arms, waist, hips, thighs, legs or feet. Remember to, **Show it! Work it! Flaunt it!** Do you Boo. Do **you!**

SIGHT. You see that certain someone across the room, at a burger stand on the street, and you want to get to know them better. Depending where you are really makes no difference, the trick is for them for them to **see** you. If you're sitting down in a restaurant, go to the ladies room making sure to pass right by them, look **directly** at them, big smile, flash them pearly whites saying "Hello." While in the ladies room, *compose yourself.* I know that he/she is cute, but breath. Palm your business card and be ready to give it to him/her when you come out. Smile, as you *slowly* pass them back to your table. This lets them know you're very interested *and* very approachable. Don't make the first move, wait for them to stop you. When they do, keep it to light small talk. Ask how their day is going so far, and mention a fun activity you enjoy. Smile, listen attentively, throw compliments at them as if they were on sale at a flea market, but make a date to meet **soon.** Now they might be shy, and you end up back at the table with your friends, but all is not lost. If that happens, as you leave, give him/her your business card. Smile, say in your most soft sexy voice, "If you're are interested, I would like the opportunity to show you how I can improve your bottom line." Yeah, yeah I know it's a bit cheesy, and they may not even own a business, but who cares. They have *your* number! The end *does* justifies the means*.

Afraid*? Too bold a move for your demure demeanor? Rather wait passively on the sidelines *hoping* they'll come to you? Well girlfriend you're going to have to get out of that comfort zone, trash the ratty bath robe, and pry the fuzzy bunny slippers out your ass! Move into the real world WOMAN THE FUCK UP! Here you are, trying to satisfy your most basic need. Sex. It's about sex. It's always about sex. Basically, you want to get **laid!** The object is to get the person to notice so you can have sex. We dress sexy, wear fragrances and makeup to attract. Otherwise, we'd just stomp around barefooted, hair uncombed in animal skins smelling like shit if it didn't matter! By the same token, if you're too afraid to approach someone to satisfy *one* of the most basic needs, sex, how in the hell are you going to satisfy the *other* basic needs? Food and housing. Basically, you want to get **paid!** A potential client holds the key to any future plans you conceive. He or she is the elusive brass ring you hope to capture as you make that journey through the corporate world to make your life a success. Get them, life is sweet, lose them, homelessness and possible starvation. It's just that simple. So suck it up, put on your big girl red panties. You've got to put yourself out there and stop being afraid. I know this is vulgar, but vulgarity is basic in the world too. *Too afraid to get laid, too afraid to get paid!*

Hearing. Hearing and Listening. There **is** a difference. When you *hear* something you notice it like a sudden movement out of the ordinary. A disturbance, a loud blaring sound that breaks the silence. When you *listen* to something you decipher it. The disturbance you've heard before is no longer a noise, but a bell or horn. You've figured it out by paying close attention. Pay close attention to *listen* to the person who is talking because…well, you'll see.

Everything you did at the restaurant, burger joint, on the street, whatever was done to perfection. You got their attention. They called! Your first phone conversation was amazing. You hadn't notice what a sweet voice this person has because the place where you'd met was so noisy, but what a sweet voice it is!!!! You become almost lost in it daydreaming floating on the sound of it. You're as giddy as a school girl and gush as they exchange a few pleasantries about you, their family, and where to meet on your date. If there was <u>ever</u> an opportunity for a girl to go shopping!!! You call yo gurrl for a day out and maybe cocktails after. You hit store after store, boutique after boutique hoping to find the perfect outfit...and you do. While driving, pointing at one of our favorite watering holes yo gurrl says, "It's hot and I'm thirsty, let's stop here and talk about this new love of yours that's got your panties all wet."

This part is not for public record. Us girls know that when we're out with yo gurrl, all conversations are to be kept private. See, told you I wouldn't tell *all*(smile).

The date was flawless! You're on cloud nine. They called you...again. You get all dolled up for your date...again. Dinner reservations at your favorite restaurant, candles, wine, perfect! The waiter clears the table and brings in the brandy. Some small talk ensues as you cup the large brandy snifter to warm it in your hands, smell it then sip. You can see that they want get to know you better, so you lean in, they do too. There's something magical about a conversation with that special someone you want to know. You want to ask them everything all at once. Looking at them, so cute, you daydream. What are your hopes your dreams? Your passions? Where do you want to live? The beach...desert... mountains? Do you like to make love? Is this the night we finally make love? Can *I* have your baby?!? You drift back to reality and say, "Are you close to your parents baby?" They say, "Uh, I was just *now* telling you baby, my parents are deceased." **A K W A R D ! ! !**

Oh no sweetie, don't look at me, I'm not going to tell you how to get out of this shit! I **told** you to *listen*. Alright, I'll tell you, later*.

Smell. Olfactory perception is the sense of smell. So important is this sense that it summons mating in the wild kingdom. In Africa known as *in heat* or *in season* it can trigger when the big cats of the Serengeti mate. Whole generations for generations has revolved around the sense of smell. Intoxicating! Arousing! Sensual! Something as powerful as smell should be treated with care, therefore, your signature fragrance should be chosen wisely. Body weight, structure, enzymes, chemicals, blood type, even medications can have a different affect on fragrances and can cause them to act differently on some. Which means, just because "Eau de Smell Good" is the bomb shit on her, doesn't mean it'll smell good on you too! The best way to find your perfect scent is to get free samples. Go to one of the big department stores' perfume counter and ask for any free samples they might have. Preferably get one that you haven't worn. Try to get as many free samples as you can without spending any money, but if you must, buy the lotion in the fragrance it cost a lot less. Wear the new fragrance for a few days to see how many compliments you get. Many compliments? People ask what are you wearing? Do they stand close to you? *That's* your signature fragrance. If it makes you sneeze, only have a few compliments, or the kids say you smell like bubblegum. Next time when you have some *me* time, fix yourself a glass of wine, dump the rest of that shit in your bath water and never use it again. Moving on!

Now that you have your signature fragrance, what *strength* is best for you?

Oil. Perfume. Cologne. Toilette.

The Big Daddy Oil is the strongest and purest form, therefore will last the longest so use it sparsely. A dab or two will do, no more. Put a dab or two in hands, rub together, distribute over entire body. If you want, can be mixed with *unscented* lotion. Oil works well with your body on long hot summer days and sexy sultry nights, because as your body heats up, so does the oil releasing it's wonderful alluring aroma!

Perfume. One step down from the long lasting big daddy oil, but it can hold its own when it comes to staying power. Best used for evenings, this aromatic accessory is best dressed up in an after five ensemble. Or dressed down with a designer bag, jeans, stiletto boots/heels or sexy strappy sandals a silk blouse and diamonds!

Cologne. Sort of the middle, but not the baby, makes her presence known when the sun is high. Break it out so you both can shine like new money, she won't let you down. You'll be a cloud of lovely fragrance as you walk by in your flouncy short dress and strappy sandals. Put a drop on the pulse points of each wrist and inside bend of elbow. Dab behind each ear, a drop on your throat, one drop on the back of your neck. When someone wants to whisper sweet nothings in your ear, tilt your head slightly forward and to the side so they can for take my full aroma, she'll do the rest. Wanna know a secret? Behind your knee, put a drop there, Shhh! There's no hair on her chest, but she's one tough cookie!

Toilette. Coy, soft, alluring, lustful beginnings The baby of the bunch but she's far from being big daddy's little angel. Yes she is the weakest one, she has no staying power, and she's always left at home while the others are in purses at the mall. She doesn't mind, home is here she is most comfortable and where she does her best work. So go on, use it up. Bathe yourself in it over your body. She's mostly alcohol so it'll dissipate quickly leaving nothing but a the light barely there fragrance. If the evening at home calls for hors d' oeuvres and cocktails, tempt and tantalize toilette is what you want. So light the candles, serve the martinis, get the whip…uh cream, lock the doors and raise some hell!

Touch. The sense of touch is found all over the body. The sense of touch originates in the bottom layer of your skin called the dermis. Ever wonder why you don't have to look behind you to know someone is there? It's because you can *feel* it. And I want to *feel* every wonderful exciting pulsating moment! Long gliding, titillating, sensuous, warm, slow, firm, loving, slightly rough but gentle, are all the adjectives I want to use to describe the hand that touches my body! Hands that know *exactly* what to do and how to tame his wild cat sexy beast. Touch me here, kiss me there, touch me *everywhere*. This is the time for some aroma therapy and a massage with warm body oils. Breakfast, lunch, dinner or a midnight snack is always the time to let me feel what makes you a man inside me. We'll spend the time finding each other's secret spot…again. That's my idea of a quiet evening, but touching can be an innocent pleasure too. It goes hand and hand with flirting when done correctly. Fluttering eyes, tossing your head back ever so slightly while running your fingers through your hair is tough to beat once you've seen a Pro do it. Don't know what I'm talking about? Ever watch old movies? Dorothy Dandridge's rhythmic hips in "Carmen". A sultry, wicked little minx that had all the boys in this man's Army standing at attention. Elizabeth Taylor's eyes. La Liz didn't have to flutter those violet beauties long to make men do her bidding. Rita Hayworth's fiery auburn hair. One sexy upward toss in the movie "Gilda", and you could see why the man in her life was willing to kill for her. Eartha Kitt. This innocent even gave Batman the blues, as the first African American Cat Woman. *Meow!* Lauren Bacall's smoky voice. What can I say? Any dame that can tame a rough neck gangster like Bogie, gets my vote every time. Those babes had **grace!**

Touch can be sensual and alluring when satisfying a lustful encounter, or calming, when it comes to reassuring a feisty child. Touch can also be used as control*. Although I can't say the product's name or use the whole marketing phrase without doling out millions, it's a great phrase. I'll give you a clue, it's the name of this section. Reach out and….. So why not call someone tonight. Too subtle?

Taste. An internal sense and pleasure. Erotica at it's best!!! Crisp Pinot Grigio, massive jumbo crab legs, luscious deep dark chocolate, iced vodka, cool frothy whipped cream, fluffy omelets, dim sum, juicy ripe red strawberries, sumptuous foie gras, tempura fried calamari, creamy cheesy lasagna, champagne, rich milk chocolate, potato au gratin, broccolini, shrimp Creole, sweet oooey gooey sticky buns, cheesy beef enchiladas, thick crisp Belgian waffles, dirty dry martinis, pineapple-carrot salad, crunchy zesty nachos, salsa, spicy gumbo, cherries flambé, warm blueberry muffins, crepes, ginger scones, rice pilaf, fizzy mimosas, hot pot stickers, snow crab, iced oyster on the half shell, smooth sweet potato pie, tender prime rib, moist lemon cream cake, bananas Foster, French apple pie, and silky chocolate mousse.

All these hot, appetite whetting, lip smacking, creamy, cheesy, mouth watering, finger licking, crunchy, sticky, juicy I don't need a napkin just let it ooze down my chin delicacies, could not be possible without your sense of taste. Catch a cold and life just isn't worth living. Wow! Taste is ***sexy!!*** Without your sense of taste, and if eating bland is all you can manage, why even eat if you can't *taste*! Brunch. One of my most **favorite** thing to do on Sunday...uh, I mean *after* Mass....well, sometimes...what I really mean is usually...uh, if I get up early enough I go to Mass...uh, wait a minute...let me start over. Do you know they serve brunch on Saturday *and* Sunday too? Yep, they do. It's my most favorite thing to do to round out the weekend. Sigh. That's better, no penance here. Hey, don't judge. Moving on!

BRUNCH. A vast array of culinary wonders for the experienced and for the not so experienced palate. This is the best time to partake of flavors that you might not have prepared for yourself at home or ordered in a restaurant. Don't be shy, taste, enjoy and have fun with the different textures, bold or subtle whimsical flavors as they dance around your mouth and tickle across your tongue. It's also *the* perfect hunting ground for a diva style in practice to bone up on her flirting skills and to partake in some yummy singles at the buffet table. I know you're hungry and you came to feed your face, but keep your options and eye out for cuties. Brunch is mostly planned for a day out for families, thus it is geared with them in mind, *but*, there's also single, working class, entrepreneurial types, hope to meet someone new and nice, corporate type, burned out at the end of the week, I just need a break and a good meal that are there too! Now, I know your hands are full with your plate, but use *that* to your advantage. Ask for help from a likely sort. You know how I said we women tend to babble? Don't do that shit here. Time is of the essence, you have to make your move quickly, the line is long, people are waiting for food or they could be married. You need answers and you need them **fast**!

First, make sure they are single by asking key questions. Looking around, say nonchalantly, "There sure are a lot of beautiful children here today. Any of them yours?" Or, be bold and aggressive. Show them your light-hearted playful side up front and say, "Can I take your picture so I can show Santa what I want for Christmas?" Short, sweet, to the point. If they oblige, they are single, *and* a damn good sport.

What a great find! If your friends don't mind and there's enough room, invite them back to your table for a drink. Or, if you don't want a crowd staring and it's better if you are alone, even better still, go to theirs. After all, it's brunch!

Tempt. Flatter. Feed with finesse. Tempt them. While at their table, lean into them. S*lowly* tilt your head to the side, slightly pucker your lips as if to invite a kiss, but don't! Then lean back, with just a hint of a devilish grin. Softly run your fingers across your mouth, down your neck, then through his hair. Lick your lips, suck *your* fingers. Flutter your eyes, hold and caress their hands.

Flatter them. Ego plays a huge role in every scenario, so always use it to your advantage. Compliment them to the point of embarrassment on their looks/ensemble/profession and/or how simply adorable you find them. Feed them. Feed their appetite with whipped cream, ruby red strawberries, sip champagne, and flirt shamelessly. It's all allowed here at brunch! *Agree* to talk later that evening to make plans for a movie, and possibly a bike ride or a day at the zoo in the near future.

Tempt. Flatter. Feed with finesse.

Now **this** is the way to a man's any damn thang you want!

Executed correctly, an afternoon brunch can be turned into a hedonistic ritual to showcase your true Diva Style.

Uh, Queen be discreet, you are in public and families are there too, so do it with... **Taste!**

CHAPTER SIX

I'M IN CONTROL

I wanted to get back to the *touch* issue as being controlling before I forget, because it is very important for you to know and remember. Men are not known for being emotional with each other unless it's with a family member or tapping each other's ass on the football field. They'll kiss mom and sis and maybe even shed a tear over the loss of a loved one, but for the most part, unlike women, emotional they are not. But boy, do they ever touch!!!

I've noticed in both business and personal world, when men and women are brought together for whatever reason there's a *touchy* game afoot. The men are always jockeying for position even if the situation didn't warrant it. A sort of tug of war domineering Alpha dog type mentality. They do this as little boys at recess on the playground, and as men during a conference meeting. Or sitting in the stands at junior's softball game, having coffee with associates, or something as simple as a non-confrontational intimate get together at a friend's home, the outcome was always the same. They touch! They touched while engrossed in very profound conversations about sports, news, naked women, the "Big Game", chicks they laid, who sucked their dick in the boardroom, naked women, the mega deal they just closed, their big swinging dicks, sports, vacations in Bimini, corner offices, pussy, 401k's stock options, all the while they touched each other. Constantly! This *touch* thing had me baffled, until I noticed it was a form of control. Another part of The Game*. This part of the Game is, for the lack of a better word, **intricate**, so pay attention.

Ok, first know this. A bad habit is a negative behavior pattern. Then, try to wrap your mind around this. Men, have a negative behavior pattern when it comes to touch. In other words, when it comes to touch, men have a bad habit. But it's not just touching, it's the *way* they touch. They place their hand on top of other's shoulder, as if told hold him down, in a subliminal jester to suggest the other to submit. It's how they *keep and hold* your attention. You got that?

Scenario. I was invited to a small impromptu party at the home of friends. I had a glass of wine and shared some polite small talk with a group of men and women. While they talk, I, sipping my drink, had noticed a man although not the host, as he moved around the room. Talking loud, laughing loud, putting his hand on the shoulders of men if attention was not paid to him. He caress each woman's back or put his arm around their waist as he exited the group, which annoyed them by their facial expression, but they smiled politely and allowed it. Then, he would let out that damn *insipid* laugh men do to show they are merely tolerating you. As he made his way to my group, the men in the group now bored, as one by one manage to slip away. There's a lull in the conversation. The obnoxious man sees this and tries to make his exit also. Clumsily, with glass in hand, he reaches for me. I don't let *any* man touch me without my permission. It's disrespectful to me as a woman, and he will learn he

does not have the right to do as he please simple because he is a man. I don't let him get away with, I love putting men in check. Shit, I relish moments like this! As he reaches for me, I take a step back from him, then tap my glass with my red nails to show him my disapproval, look him *directly* in his eyes, and sternly say, "I don't tolerate idiots either. They'll drag you down to their level, and beat the **hell** out of you with their experience." Lifting one eyebrow, I walk away from him!

End Scenario

Can you just imagine the dumbfounded look on his face? As Professional Woman, other than a handshake, under **no** circumstance will touching will be tolerated dammit! Turn the tables on those bastards. Let them know it's a new day and there's a new sheriff in town. Speak Up. Be Aggressive. Be Strong. Be Creative. Attributes needed if you are ever going to succeed. Don't be some mealy mouth slack jawed pussy afraid to speak up for yourself or too scared to jump in with both feet. Take that leap of faith and woman up! Say it with me my queen. Game going on *everywhere*! I am **KANG BITCH!**

Someone ruffled your feathers in the *business* aspect of your life? Don't gossip with your girlfriends or others in the office about it, put them fuckers in check! Work within the system. Nip it in the bud by following the chain of command. Schedule a meet with your Supervisor, the head of Human Resource, and the offending perpetrator(s). Take notes in the meeting and make sure to have it documented.

Put a copy of the grievance in *their* employee's record folder, and I'll bet you won't have any problems with them again.

Want a raise? Owed one? Stand up, be aggressive! Stay overtime when and if allowed or do extra work for other staff members a month or two **before** you ask for a raise. Always stay busy, never idle. Ask for tedious, time consuming assignments. Make sure the key players, like your immediate boss, Office Manager, Supervisor etc. sees this. When the time comes, schedule a meet. Bring in all the completed assignments, and overtime. Express your love for the company, it's products, staff and your tenure with the firm. Lastly, give your percentile increase, and thank them for their time. Now, you may or may not get a raise, but at least this shows them you are willing to go the extra mile in order to achieve. It also shows them that you know there's a game going on and you know how to play *and* win! But if you feel you are unappreciated, underpaid, or just plain old spinning your wheels and another firm down the line will better serve you, by all means...

move the fuck on Boo!

Maybe you're tired of the corporate world, and you want a new adventure. Starting your own business can be exciting. Be strong. There's a lot of decisions to make! Brick and mortar? Online? What do I sell? Cosmetics? Perfumes? Bath crystals? OH HELL THE FUCK NO!!!! This is harder than I thought, but whatever the merchandise, I'm up for the challenge. I have to do this...and I can't forget about that.... I've got to go downtown to get my business license tomorrow.

I've settled on a product, the website took a little longer than expected because I had to build it myself. Have to save money you know, but it's ok. It's been several months, the business is doing fair, and my computer froze on me. Completely. I called a tech, he said,

"It'll cost $25.00 to come out and *look* at the computer and $25.00 every hour I'm there." "WHAT the fu..!?! Are you shitin' me?"

"No ma'am."

"Fine, you've got me over a barrel I don't have a choice, I need my computer for my work."

45 damn minutes later, this snotty nose kid walks in my door looking all of 17 but was actually 28 (because I asked), fixed my computer in 2 minutes flat, and said

"That'll be $50.00 ma'am." without blinking an eye!

"What?!? What did you do?"

"Well ma'am I…"

He might as well be explaining it in Greek because that's just how well I understood what he said. He watched as I wrote the check just as closely as he watched me since he came in the door. Then give it to him I saying,

"Was it good for you?"

"Was it good for me?"

I finished coyly, "Yeah, 'cause **one** of us got screwed!"

He falls out laughing, then smiled saying,

"I like older women."

Sternly I look into his fresh, young unassuming wide eyes and say,

"So do I."

Out done, he leaves. I guess it wasn't *that* funny after all! I can't have this wide eyed young buck camped out on my porch thinking there maybe some chance to be with me. I read him when he first rode up, and I had to cut him off at the knees. And that's the way to do it! Oh, for the record, and so there's no misunderstanding, **I'm strictly dickly!**

I can't believe it's almost been a year since I started my business. Sales are not where I projected, but that's fine. What I need is to be projected on top of a fine man! Shit can't think about that now, I've got to get supplies. I check the mail. Damn is it almost time to renew my license again? Pay taxes? How can I *owe* when I didn't make a fuckin' dime? I don't feel well. Is that a cold coming on? I can't get sick now, I don't have any medical. Light bill. Why is it so high? Gotdamn computer sucking up all the energy *and* the life out of me. Gas bill. Car note, rent. Calgon take me away! *I am* **KANG BITCH** dammit! I'm tired of putting lipstick on this pig and trying to sell it. I need a job…with benefits! Back into the corporate world I go. Shit! Shit!

Be creative. I updated my resume to show me as a new business owner for the past year. That should bolster it up! Right? Nnnope! After several interviews with different companies I was sure I had in the bag, they felt that I was "over qualified" for the position. *Over qualified!?!* Can you believe that? I want to know how, and when, does a person become over qualified? Is there a gage hidden somewhere in Human Resource that measures this? Show me the contraption that says I went over the limit! If there is one dammit, I want to see it. Where is it stated that I am certified as "over qualified" across the board? Every fuckin' body is telling me that! What's the limit? At what range did I exceed it?! My last job? The one before? Being born female? Who in the bloody hell made up this phrase and why do we put up with it? You are either qualified or you're not qualified. Aw shit, here we go again. Some of that right wrong, left right, it's either black white shit! It's like saying, no thank you, I've had enough to eat, I'm *over full*. Or, I'd better get up, I can't sleep another wink, I'm *over rested*. Sigh, the men strike again. I removed the business from my resume and explained the gap as being *under employed* to be funny, but that didn't go over well on my last interview. I changed it to being unemployed, which was a lie. I *was* employed. I had a damn *business*. This shit is STUPID! The Game. It's all part of *their* fuckin' game! Ladies, are you tired of this shit??

ARE YOU TIRED *YET*??!!!!

I need some sleep. I have another interview tomorrow.

When I walked into the office, I already *knew* I had the job. I know the game, I know how to play, this time, I came to win! Dressed to the nines, I was open for business. My hair tastefully worn up and away from my face so they can see my eyes and sincerity, light makeup for daytime and a blush of red tinted lipstick. Nails cut just above the tip of my fingers polished in a coral hue. Cream cashmere skirt and sweater set, bone colored closed in one inch leather heels, stockings, multi-color tan bone and red Coach bag and black attaché case completed my ensemble. I can't explain it, but it was a confidence engulfed my whole being. Self assured, confident, with just a hint of cockiness was displayed by me as I took my seat, and crossed my legs at the ankles with the interviewer. For a change, this time, it was a female. I studied her face as I sat, so I drew back some of my cockiness. Question after question hurtled at me as if in some championship tennis match. She's impressed. She talked about the firm, it's products and her expectations of me. We discuss pay schedules, stock options, 401k's and salaries. As I remember, *everything is negotiable*, we negotiate my salary up front*. She smile and agree to my terms. I accept the position. Now the ball is in my court when she asks, "When can you start?" I say, "Yesterday." Now, ***I'm in control!***

Finally some medial benefits! Going back into the corporate world was not my idea of living life to its fullest, but a girls' gotta do what a girls' gotta do. Having my own business, being my own boss and being on my own has its upside…

and downside. Yes it was fulfilling, yes it was exciting, but you must understand that all the burden falls on your *hopefully* capable shoulders. You are now the chief cook and bottle washer if you are your company's **only** employee. Bookkeeper? Hope you know about spreadsheets and how to balance your in and out columns when the IRS comes a calling. Know how to be an Office Manager? How to order Logo pens, printer paper, toner etc.? Going to the local drug store or office supply won't do, you'll need to buy in bulk to meet your demands now! You'll need a fax machine too, one that is *separate* from your land line. Did you know that? Me neither, you could've knocked my ass over with a feather too! You'll need a Marketing Representative!! Do you know how to market your product get a "buzz" started?!!? Do you have a focus group?!? Do you know where/how to get one?!! Get a targeted audience?!? A Mission Statement?!! LLC or Corporation???!! Tax ID number?!!? Data Backup!! Business License?! EIN number?!!? This is just to START the business!! Erasers?!!? Fax! Absolut?!!! Grey Goose?!!! Dry martini, vodka or gin? Am I out of my mind?!! What the fuck was I thinking!!!???

The upside is being your own boss, downside no one to blame but yourself if it fails. But you know, I don't feel that I've failed, I look at it as a learning experience. One I will **never ever** attempt again! That's the whole point of life. To jump out there get your feet wet. *Try.* You'll never know what might happen by passively sitting on the sidelines watching and waiting for shit to happen. Nothing beats a fail but a try! I found that this was not my calling that's all. I'm a leader, but not at this, so I'll try something else. Maybe if I have some down time, I'll try my hand at writing and see where that takes me! (smile) Be in control of your *own* destiny. Just like this book, think of it as a buffet. A wide array of titillating morsels, select what suits your appetite, and leave the rest for someone else to savor.

We're gonna switch gears for a minute, but it's still about *you,* being in control.

A LIVING WILL

This can be an unpleasant subject for some us, but one we must brooch with the utmost concern and urgency. A Living Will. Do you have one in place? A Living Will is a form of advance directive leaving instructions for treatment. It authorizes a specific person to more or less to have power of attorney on your behalf if and when we become incapacitated. In other words, if you want your final wishes followed verbatim, put it in writing!

Our family, God Bless 'em, the backbone of existence that is you. If you were blessed to have a been raised in a place that love dwelled, then you know of where I speak. Maybe it was a place that was created for you, or built by you. Single story or two, duplex or tri, big city lights, or easy country living, suburbs. North, South, East, or West. No matter what type of a home that you were born into one that was created for you or built by you, it's all equally blessed by family. Our children whom you've cared so much for, and have protected all their lives, can now be in jeopardy if there is nothing in writing specifying who gets what. Something as simple as a cotton tablecloth you got at yard sale for a lousy buck, can be a silly heated issue between the kids if both wants it. I have had the misfortune and been privy to firsthand knowledge of how loving, caring family members can be turned into a vicious pack wolves, once their loved ones have gone onto glory. Though some liberties were taken, a few precautions were exercised to protect the stupid…I mean intelligent-challenged adults. I'm trying very hard to be politically correct, but I'm use to speaking my mind and being brutally honest. Sigh. Don't judge. Moving on!

After the serene funeral of a loved one was over, some of my family and I gathered outside my aunt's over crowded house on the front lawn. All these beautiful familiar and unfamiliar faces glowed in the afternoon Bayou sun, as we talked about our loss and got to know each other better. It's been years since we've seen each other, so we reminisce about old times. "Baby", my uncle says as the crowd listens, "I remember your mother use to fix your plate, and you didn't like your food touching. I thought it was the cutest, but the oddest thing! Are you still like that?"

Looking around the group I say, "Of course not."

Funny how he can turn me back into that shy girl! The cousins I'm closer with now join the group and conversations. My cousin's wife says to my female cousin,

"I see you are wearing the diamond necklace we gave your mom for Mother's Day last year."

Now, holding it between her fingers, she nods.

"We paid a lot of money for the necklace. I was wondering if we could have it back?"

!!!!!!!!!!!!!!!! Talk about a jaw-dropping moment!!! That was my reaction because words **cannot** describe the face I had when she said that! My dear, sweet, delightful, well informed, woman in the *know* cousin did not answer. Instead, with an abhorrent look, she looked down at her feet, then back to her face, lifted the diamond necklace to her lips, kissed it, and walked away! I couldn't help myself, I didn't say it out loud, but under my breath, I said BRAVA BITCH!!! I could not have been more proud of her! You see, it was her mother's funeral. Her mother is my mother's younger sister. The training that was giving to me by my mother, was obviously given to my female cousin, by *her* mother. The apple doesn't fall far from the tree! A puzzled look was now apparent on my cousin's wife face from no training at all. Now I'm trying hard not to laugh in her face and pointing to my cousin's 'kiss my ass walk-away' said,

"*That* means no, you can't have it!"

So, if you want little Mookie to have your spatula, but you don't want cousin Trevor's nasty mouth no where near mamma's favorite spoon, put that shit in a Living Will!

401k's CONTRIBUTION. Money, money, money. The root of all evil. Really? Who said that? I smell a rat… I mean a man. Same thing you say? Hummm maybe. Anyway, money is not the root of all evil. The *lack* of it is. **Negotiate**

your salary up front! We as women are never going to be paid what we are worth, or the same as a man. You have to go in another way. Do you know they have a scale for the position depending on gender at the Executive Level? Negotiate your salary up front. Ever heard of a glass ceiling? Economics? Projected Quotas? Negotiate your salary up front! Once you become employed, check to see if the company has a 401k plan in place. If so, it would behoove you to contribute to this program. Once fully vested(usually after five years of service)the company will match you dollar for every dollar contributed. Check with IRS Resource Guide for general rules and dollar amounts for your age group. If you're over 50, these amounts can accelerate called a *catch up* contribution. It's nice to have an IRA or a ROTH too. Keep it separate from your regular checking/saving accounts preferably at a different bank so it won't so be readily available to dip into.

ONLINE BILL PAY *or* **AUTOMATIC BILL PAY.** Which one you choose is up to you. Online gives you control to pay a bill at your leisure, or to fit your pay schedule. The only draw back I see is you could forget to pay the bill *and* incur late penalties, therefore screw up your credit rating.

Automatic bill pay, set up once by you, is deducted automatically from your checking at a specified time of each month. It's convenient and saves time, ***but*** make sure to keep up with the payment schedules. Determine if it is a *definite* payment bill like utilities. A land line, rent or cell phone where the bill goes on and on month by month and is never paid off.

Timed payment bills like car or house notes. Payments after a certain allotted time, will cease to exist. God forbid you have an accident and laid up in traction for a year. You're two months away from paying off your car or house note. Guess what? If no one has your computer password, or changes are not made to your bank, those payments are still **on going** Sporty! Month after month after month, year after year. And trust, a computer is not going to call and say a mistake has been made and you're sending *too much money!*

Be sure to keep your passwords in a safe place. If it's on your computer, keep it locked with a password only you and a trusted other knows. Preferably the one with power of attorney.

Sticky situations can and *will* occur at any given time. You don't want this to be one of them. I'm **CONTROL** of me!

CHAPTER SEVEN

STICKY SITUATIONS

According to Wikipedia, hoof and mouth disease is an infectious and sometimes fatal viral disease that affects cloven hoofed animals including domestic and wild bovid. The virus causes high fever for two or three days, followed by blisters inside the mouth and on the feet that may rupture and can cause lameness.

WOW! I knew a couple of bitches that fits that description. Hoof and mouth disease. Except, this time around, we will refer to this lesson as

Foot in Mouth Disease.

We've all had these unpleasant sticky situations where we just rather get back the moment. You know, we've said or done something **really** stupid. Your mouth drops open suddenly in horror, your face gets hot and turns red. You want to crawl back under the covers in bed, get a do over, become I dream of Jeannie and blink it away, or pray to God Almighty they didn't hear the blunder that just fell out of your mouth! You can't *believe* you just said what you've just said. A Freudian slip some might call it. If you've had too much to drink, you'd say it was the alcohol, or if you've been a bad girl like Flip Wilson's flamboyant sassy character "Geraldine", you'd say, the devil made me do it. Or THE worse offense one can commit, character assentation. Shot yourself in the foot. Painted yourself into a corner. Whatever the culprit, the damage is done. You can't unring a bell. You've dug yourself into a hole by saying or doing the wrong thing, or by simply not close paying attention. How do I get out of this?

Well, it's very simple. First of all, don't panic! A **KANG BITCH!** is *always* in control. The sun is still going to rise in the East, up is still up, down is still down, left is opposite of right and the world is not going to suddenly end because you've contracted *foot in mouth disease.* It depends on the situation. *Decipher* first, then *control.* Did you *say* something wrong? Or did you *do* something wrong because you weren't paying attention? In order to take control of a situation my Alpha personalities, you must be even more masterful. More aggressive. Nor is this is not the time to be a wallflower, or a passive sideliner. You all must grow some imaginary balls*! Face it, you fucked up, and you have to drag your cookies out the fire.

Please refer to the Chapter Five FLIRTING subject HEARING. Of course change the family member's name where it applies when necessary. Why are you looking puzzled? Did you forget? Remember I said I'll tell you later? You know, the breadcrumb*? *Do you remember the breadcrumb?* Sigh. For those with short term memory or memory loss, please incorporate some vitamin B-12 into your diet! In the meantime, and for the rest of you, I'll copy and paste because we don't have time for you to go back and *read it dammit*! I'm sorry, I didn't mean to offend you. Kiss. Feel better now?

Ok, this is where we left off, ... "Are you close to your parents baby?" They say, "Uh, I was just telling you baby, my parents are deceased." **A K W A R D!!** Remember now? Ok. *MOVING ON!!!!!!!!!!!!!!!*

If you've **said** something wrong. While holding their hand lovingly, look **directly** into their eyes. In your most sincere, heart wrenching, soft, and venerable voice say,

"Yes baby, I know you said you're parents are deceased, mine are too, but I'm still close to them. What I mean is, quite often in my alone time, or when I'm feeling blue, I talk to them and draw them in, close to me. Then I don't feel so all alone anymore. So in a way, I'm still close to my parents. Do you know what I mean sweetheart?"

Clutch the pearls! Awww, you poor, poor baby! Sniff, sniff! Anybody got a tissue?

You know what type response you're going to get? A DAMN GOOD ONE! Wanna know why? *Carefully worded words!* Forget that it's doesn't matter *what* you say it's *how* you say it bullshit, because that's exactly what it is, bullshit. That's what untrained women say to confuse women. Don't fall victim to that. It **does** matter *what* you say, just as much as *how* you say it. Carefully worded words*. In the above skit you are letting them know, before you met them, your evenings were lonely and for the most part you were blue. You needed comfort, and are reaching out to fill a void. If they are an astute suitor, they will pick up on this and quickly rectify the situation. Since you weren't paying attention, you humble yourself and offer loving attention by holding their hand. Make sure to repeat the last sentence you heard clearly, and make your deductions from there adding a term of endearment such as, "Yes *baby*, I know you said…." Incorporate the *foot in mouth* incident into a touching story. You don't want to leave them guessing what to say next, so *always, always* end with a question for their feed back, **plus** another term of endearment. Silence is golden. Wait for their answer. This will keep the conversation flowing, and not leave an uncomfortable silence.

And the Oscar goes to…

If you've **done** something wrong.

Oooo child, that's whole 'nother animal! It's hard to back peddle your way out of deep shit. We're going to have to do some fast talking here, so put some tomatoes in your shoes and ketchup. Sorry. Where do I start? Humm, I'm gonna need a stiff one for this! Excuse me while I fix a dry martini. What were *you* thinking? You silly, but…I love a dirty mind!

Hi, I'm back, sorry for the inconvenience. I've given great thought to this, and there is only one way to handle this. One, you can moan and groan, say it was due to some out of body experience or was medically induced. Cramps, hot flashes, *that* time of the month, dog ate my homework. My shoes are too tight, I broke my heel, or, my favorite, my grandmother died and I have to attend the funeral. Water weight gain, my diet isn't working…again, low sugar, I'm lactose intolerant, little Timmy's stuck in the well, my fuckin' biological clock is ticking louder than Big Ben, the pipe broke and the plumber didn't show up and what have you. Are you shit'n me? Those tactics are not to be used… Unless absolutely positively necessary!(smile) Besides, they *saw* you do the deed, therefore those excuses are null and void. Or two, you can grow some balls* the size of walnuts, pull up your pretty red panties and own up to your mistake. It's **the** logical thing to do. Tell them emphatically the mistake was yours. As before, change the name where it applies. Let's keep in mind you are a **KANG BITCH!** Stand firm on your convictions. In a soft voice with shoulders slightly rounded, as you enter the room, show self torture in your eyes say…

"Sir/Madam, the decision was made to move forward on the project only after countless hours of tedious research had been conducted by me. Apparently, I must have overlooked something in my notes. I assure you in the future, I will not be so Avant-garde in my writing. I ask that you forgive my boorish behavior."

It wasn't your fault!!! Some son of a bitch set you up!!!! Sniff, sniff!! Anybody got a tissue?

Wow! You snatched them cookies out the oven just in time! They were just about to get burned! Carefully worded words* can save the day. Careful. I didn't say *will,* save the day, I said *can,* save the day. Another carefully worded word example. Pay close attention to that when speaking to someone or when someone speaks to you. It'll save you in the long run.

Back to our little skit. Wow you snatched them cookies… anyway you get the jest.

The first thing you do is stand firm on your convictions. Same as before, you fucked up, so right the wrong. The rounded shoulders, is a subliminal tactic to show submission, and a way of asking for their acceptance to your apology. The self tortured look displayed in your eyes is to show you have already deciphered the problem, and have beat yourself up severely about it before you got to them. You tell them that even though your actions were wrong, it was done through countless hours of research. Therefore, any miscalculations on your part, which can *now* be attributed to human error is a strong possibility. And as we **all** know, to err is human. Am I moving too fast? Ketchup! Then, you follow up with a *brilliant* show of breeding by using(correctly I might add) that certain je ne sais qua, in reference to your notes as being *Avant garde*. As you know, an Avant garde way of writing means free wheeling or having an innovative way of thinking. Who even **know** to do that? Then, without hesitation or shame, you throw yourself at their mercy, and ask for forgiveness. Shit! Now *that's* fucking class!(Oops! Sorry). That's a **KANG BITCH!** Next time pay attention, because the only sticky situation you should be involved in is warm honey and your Sweetie!

You'd say, how can I pay attention to wardrobe, how I eat, think on my feet, *and* listen to what's said, flirting etc.? That's a lot to remember! Yes it's a lot to remember but I'd say, as time goes by implementing all the new techniques, it will come as second nature. You'll wear them like a warm comfortable terrycloth robe and feel secure confidence. Just like you learned old habits, learning new ones are done the same way, a little at a time. Move with slow consistent steps everyday. Incorporate a new element like wearing red, which is an absolute must, being more aggressive, tips on flirting, makeup etc., or any topics we've talked about and *keep it* in your daily routine. You didn't become the personality you are overnight, by the same token, learning to be a strong, independent woman is going to take time. Don't become overwhelmed or think I can't do this because it's too hard. Hell, if it were easy, every woman would be a **KANG BITCH!** but they're not.

But that's what makes the world go 'round, different people with different backgrounds with different outlooks on life. Some leaders, some followers. I love the eclectic mix*, it feeds my soul. To be a leader, takes special attention to detail and carries a great deal of responsibility. In order to be a leader, you must have followers or else what's the point, but you must also be able to show compassion.

CHAPTER EIGHT

FOLLOW ME!

Children and their backyard shenanigans. "It's my ball, and you have to play my game!" Sticking out their tongue with thumb in their ears waving their fingers singing nana na nana! Something a child would say, right? As a child, if they said that to you, you'd let the air out of their ball, or beat 'em up, and take their ball. Yeah, that's mature! Then they would say, "Gimme my ball, you're not the boss of me!" Hold on, not so fast pal. That's exactly what we do as adults!

Please. Thank you. Excuse me. What ever happened to common decency!? What ever happened to good manners? In this world, good manners seem to have become passé. We were taught good manners as children, but as we grew, we forgot and became rude, manipulative abrasive adults. In a sense, we've become bullies. Cliques of deviants find the weakest amongst you in the workplace, prey on them as a hungry animals in the wild, and attack. But they don't do it for food like the animals in the wild, it's done for sport! They pounce on the poor unsuspected victim who is venerable or naïve, and begin the assault.

An office clique can have a negative effect on your relationship with your Management team. Gathering at the water cooler or around the *it* girl's desk for a little impromptu conference about last evening night maneuvers, or Sally Sue's sad excuse for that hideous outfit she's wearing today sends those lips a flapping! Loose lips sinks ships, and here comes Sally Sue sailing into their muddy waters when the giggles ensue. Like a bunch of unruly teenage schoolgirls, they point, taunt and harass as she passes by. Sally Sue is not a threat to them, just some passive ordinary office worker that does her job and minds her *own* business. Poor Sally Sue has no way of knowing she is the butt of their jokes, smiles politely at them, and goes on with her day. The girls ask Sally Sue to lunch only to further torment her. Unknowingly, poor thing, she accepts. This sort of adolescent behavior can continue on and on for days, weeks and maybe even years without Sally Sue knowing. Women act in this manner when cliques are formed, and can be detrimental to the work place. You might ponder the thought, isn't Sally Sue their best worker? Question asked. Question answered!

Being a part of the corporate world for such a long time, I've had my share of different managers. Bosses of all nationalities, various ethnic backgrounds, straight, gay, good, bad, indifferent, male and female. I'm shame to say, the females were the least liked.

Not just by me, but by all in the office. I don't know if it's because we were of liked sex, waking up on the wrong side of no man in the morning, or bitch had a wild hair up her ass. All I know is, if dealing with an office full of women, you're in for some catty drama and jealousy. The health care profession is the worse, because here is where it is predominantly female. To get around this particular problem, I will give you some more examples on how to dress for success. Business casual is the *new norm* uniform in the workplace.

Why is it when women get a meaty position, they either go from one extreme to another? They act like a sophomoric school girls with a new crush, all giddy and shit. Oh Mr. Big Ol' Strong Man, I am so grateful for the opportunity you just afforded me to work in this great big 'ol company. I don't know how little 'ol me is going to do, but I'm so happy to be here!! Or, butch up their act. Hey, whassup dawg, where's the can? Just kidding!!! They tend to dress like they *think* a man wants a woman to dress if he were a woman, suited down, losing their femininity, and act like them. Head strong, tough as nails, no room for errors and showing no compassion. Can't we find a happy medium?

Now there's nothing wrong with a woman dressed in well tailored suit. In fact, I find it's quite sexy! As long as it's done correctly. Thank goodness, with women's suits, we are offered far more options than males. Big bold vibrant colors! More colors than you can shake a dick…uh, I mean stick at. Suit colors they can't get away with in the workplace, but we can wear and look fierce! Bright pink and lemon yellow! Ruby red and emerald green! Vibrant oranges and purples! Just from those colors alone, you can go from one end of the spectrum to the other and the men still, in the words of MC Hammer, "Can't touch this!" You can always fall back on your muted or standard colors like black, greys or charcoals, blues, and browns. There's also an array of whimsical patterns, cuts, sleeve lengths, and a variety of bottoms that can be added instead of their ever present trouser. An "A" line, long/short, or pencil skirt can also be worn. Adding a lacy camisole or semi sheer blouse under a button down blazer is very chic. If there's a client meet or dinner engagement after, you can remove the blazer and toss on a long string of faux pearls or sparkling rhinestone necklace. On Fridays, maybe denim can worn, but check with your Human Resource as to their policies. Look in the mirror, try on different colors, you know what works best for you. Just do you Boo. *Do you!*

Think before you ink. This is a phrase you should familiarize yourself with in the corporate world. It's my way, or the highway. How many times have you heard this terminology? This shit can blow up in your face.

"Madam, I have been with the firm for over five years now. I have never been late and always completed assignments large or small. When asked, I've worked overtime, forgo lunches and trained my subordinates whom have since moved on to higher positions. I have kept quite in the process because I needed this job. I feel this is not working out for me. If things don't change soon, I might have to render my resignation."

DAMN! Sounds like somebody *wants* to get fired!

If I were your boss, and you sashayed your hot ass into my office with that attitude, you'd leave me no alternative. I wouldn't accept your resignation. I'd fire you! How dare you give me an ultimatum?!? *I'm* the fuckin' boss! Another prime example of carefully worded words. If you go in there with the thought of the boss has got to see things *your* way, you're bucking for a place in line at the unemployment office

Pookie! Wasn't what you had in mind when you went in there? You just wanted to talk right? Maybe even scare her a little. Thought you had the juice huh? Well, we certainly are full of ourselves aren't we? You didn't go in there with the *thought* of getting fired? Really!?! Tell me you didn't see that shit coming! In the corporate world, you've just done(and quite well I might add)to *yourself,* do what no one else could possibly do. **The** greatest crime of all. You've committed your own CHARECTER ASSENATION. Maybe your boss was searching for an avenue to get rid of you and this was her way out. Not only did you give her the gun, but you supplied the target and ammo! Way to go.

It's obvious you're upset and fed up, but unless you have a more lucrative job waiting in the wings, the most you can do is bite the bullet, so to speak. You don't have to be head strong or tough as nails to get your point across. If you go in her office with guns a blazing, not leaving her wiggle room to make any compensations, acting like a spoiled child, giving ultimatums if things don't change, you *will* get fired! Essentially you're saying, I'm taking my ball and going home! Sound vaguely familiar? That's being childish on your part. Well sugar, this is **not** the backyard, and you are no longer a child. This is the *real* world with *real* adult problems, and those backyard shenanigans aren't going to fly here. You can't stomp, take your ball home, or hold your breath till your face turns blue. All those "extras" you so eloquently mentioned in your little speech that you did are a part of your job. You are their corporate mule. Their do as I say do, jump when I say jump, lift that barge, tote that bale, get me some coffee, wash that dish, kiss my ass girl.

Training, working overtime etc. is what is *expected* of you. Don't want to do it? Someone else will at a lessor cost. The boss knows it, Management knows it and sadly now, so do you. Next time you decide to go in unknowingly to **slit your own throat**, have your ducks in a row. It's all part of the game. This time you played…and *lost!*

I know it can be difficult to retain, and I've given you a shit load to remember, but try this.

Football has rules that are different than baseball, and basketball rules are different from tennis but they *all* involve a balls. Games have **balls***. Different rules apply to every game. It's all a game, but the rules are *different*. When dealing with a **female** boss, it's much different than dealing with a **male** boss. It involves three key factors.

1. Calm down
2. Have a cooler demeanor
3. Don't focus on the negative

Although you would treat her with the same respect as you would a male boss, a certain amount of FINESSE should be used. Don't be so combative, this is not a contest. With **her,** play the game*of sensitivity. You need to earn her trust, so she'll be more receptive to your ideas. Offer your suggestions, then ask for hers. If you have suspicions regarding your performance, first ask if she's unhappy, and suggest ways for you to improve. Female bosses tend be more *detailed oriented* than males, so ask questions about how she want the work completed. One female boss I had liked the completed spreadsheet printed out, then put in her inbox at the end of every business day, another wanted it emailed. When she gives you an idea, **use it.** Let her know you are trustworthy and how much you appreciate her skills. Be her go-to or right-hand person always on-call whenever the need arise. I know it sounds like I'm asking you to be an ass kisser, but you need to build a trust, create a bond with her *if* you want her in your corner. She is trying harder, just like you are, because of her position. She has to be three and sometime four times better than a man, when it come to managing a team of office workers. She has a lot on her plate, show her some consideration, there's enough wealth to go around. If you allow her the opportunity, she has the juice to make recommendations in your favor, boost your salary, offer information for-your-ears-only to help you to succeed. Playing the game of sensitivity can be tricky. You can end up being her 'lap dog' if she's a greedy game player so, always keep your guard up. Be bold, be confident, be the aggressor, with *finesse!*

The days for showing no compassion, being tough as nails, beating our chests like some maniac and acting like a spoiled child are over. We are going to go back to the beginning where good manners prevailed. Our nature dictates it. A place where we care what happens to each other, stop acting like crabs in a barrel, standing on the backs of other's in order to reach the top.

"Please can you direct me to Ms. Domino's office? Thank you. Excuse me, is this Ms. Domino's office? Yes, may I help you? Thank you for your assistance, I appreciate it. Excuse me, can you tell me where I can find the… Thank you. Excuse me. May I help you? Thank you for your assistance, I appreciate it. Excuse me, can you tell me where I can find the"….And tell them!

How hard is that to do? We are the first teachers of Generations for all Generations. We all were taught good manners as children, but somewhere along the way we forgot. To be a leader you don't have to be an elected official. Maybe you are a good problem solver, one who inspires, knows how to develops one's talents, or offers good advice. I consider myself the latter. Ladies, we as intelligent grown ass Diva Style women have got to stop being so greedy, catty and selfish. There's enough wealth to go around. We are no longer bullies.

Know this. The end result, *does* justifies the means, on how we got there. We all, as powerful intelligent women with power and in the know, *can* have it all.

I'm not claiming to be a leader, yours or anyone else's, but I will show compassion and ask for your assistance when following these instructions and say…Please adhere.

Thank you. I appreciate.

CHAPTER NINE

THE "OTHER" TALK

In the beginning, God Created heaven and earth. He Created Man. He Created Woman. God help us!

Ever since Eve took a bite from the forbidden fruit, she set in motion out fate. We cannot outrun destiny. Women are destine to bring forth children. In order to do this, certain changes in our bodies must and will take place. As for every time there is a season, and every season brings about a change. The change in our season brings about a season of birth. Since the beginning of time, it occurs like clockwork, a woman's natural body functions. Nothing stops it, nothing hinders it. A death, taxes, economics, come hell or high water, it happens to all born female. Ain't it funnnnn being a woman*?

We've all had that "talk" with our mother's or some other female when we were girls about the birds and the bees. My mother sat my brother and I down when I was nine, and he was ten. I thought it was **THE** most God awful thing a man could do to a woman! I couldn't imagine it, "You mean to tell me she *lets* him do that to her!?!" Before "the talk", I thought if a family had two or three children, that's how many times they had *did it*, and was happy to believe that! Yeah I know, I was very young and very naïve. Then, if that wasn't enough, alone with mother later that day, you couldn't believe my horror when she told me about menstruation. That's nasty! I said no way is this gonna happen to me, I'm not gonna let it! Of course it did a few years later no matter how much I tried to pray it away.

I started in the early '60's when there were only two choices. Tampax or Kotex. Tampax extra absorbent blue box were for adult women. The Tampax you had to INSERT INSIDE YOU. A twelve year old. Sticking that in me!?! Are you kidding?!? Kotex in the cutesy Pepto Bismol pink color box for teens. At first, they had those damn elastic belts that came in the box, but for some reason the manufactures stop supplying them. You'd wear it around your waist like a belt next to your skin, it had a metal loop that the cloth wings on the pad would fit through, then attached to this huge pad between you and your panties front *and* back. How comfy! I'd walked around during my time of the month looking like I just got off a horse. It was awful! Wow, some choice! I'd asked, "How long is this gonna last?" Mother tells me thirty five or forty years, maybe longer, maybe shorter, it depends. **WHAT!?** *It Depends?* Depends on what?

MENOPAUSE!!!! Hot flashes, hormonal changes, vaginal dryness, mood swings, irregular periods, memory loss, night sweats, difficulty sleeping, painful intercourse, irritability, unexplained weight gain. Menopause literally means the end of your monthly cycle. Pause of menses. Menses, periodic flow of blood. Phonetically, MEN O PAUSE.

Enough of the technical terminology, let's get real. Literally it's more like **bitch** on wheels!

1946 to 1964 was the largest population explosion ever! Baby Boomers. More and more of female Baby Boomers are reaching senior maturity. It has not gone unnoticed by me, that the advertising market has been gearing up for years with a huge influx of products. The drug and cosmetic industries are going to make billions upon billions, off the narcissistic behavior of my generation to look younger.

Of all the subjects mother and I discussed, we never got a chance to talk to about this one. This is the 'other' talk, the no one wants to discuss. More dreaded than the "curse", as referred to as our periods by our mothers, menopause has become a hush-hush* controversial subject. I don't know why this is such a taboo* subject amongst women since at some point in our lives, we all eventually inter into this. I will however shed some light on this because, I **love** discussing subjects that are taboo, hush-hush and controversial!

First of all, I don't want to alarm you but, **AAAHHHH!** Sorry, but I had to let that scream out to release some pinned up emotions. That's the great thing(ha ha)about menopause, it forces you to show emotions when you least expect it. Your world is so out of whack, you start to doubt your own sanity. Snapping at people for no reason, and crying uncontrollably. Or, imagine it's a comfortable sixty-nine degrees outside, you're home alone* watching your favorite TV program. As sweat drips down your face, neck and bosom as if someone had turned on a hose, you ask out loud, **"WHY IS IT SO FUCKIN' HOT IN HERE!?!"** *to no one.* Or, you wonder, to yourself, my keys. Where are my keys? I just had them a minute ago. Who moved my keys? For the next half hour, you go bananas searching all over the house for your keys. Under the couch, in the closet, behind the chair. You even looked in the freezer, because once(yeah, I know, don't judge)I found them in there. Where could they be? I gotta sit down. *Think! Think!* Where did I last have them? I had to have them to drive myself home. I had to have them to get in the house. I'm *inside*. What did I do with them after that? Shit! Shit! Suddenly, a light bulb goes off. Oh no the hell I **didn't!!!** You go to the back door, and lo and behold, wouldn't you just know it, the missing keys are dangling in the door…on the *outside!* It had been there **ALL NIGHT LONG!!!!** I could've been violated. It's a good thing I live in a secured building with a ten foot fence around the property. I was so shaken by the thought of what might have happened I was beside myself. This menopause shit was not going to be the death of me. I'm an intelligent woman, and I knew how to research problems, so I did. I found some women will develop symptoms in their late thirties or early forties, or fifties, while others will sail through without any need for medications, herbal remedies or a vodka martini. The good thing is, most women will experience few symptoms. To those I say, **BRAVA BITCH!** I'm not apologizing I am menopausal! For the rest, here are some suggestions.

To minimize hot flashes, eat less spicy foods, control your alcohol and caffeine intake. When choosing an outfit for the day or evening, dress in layers. You'll be getting hot *and* cold more often now, so save the Toots LaRue stripe tease act for Sweetie. Oh, while we're on the subject of stripping, for vaginal dryness* KY jelly helps. Use a little desk fan at work or at home, and take deep slow breaths when you feel a flash coming on. Herbal remedies like black cohosh are good, but note are not a quick fix if you are in dire need. If all else fails, check with your female doctor for some HRT(Hormone Replacement Therapy).

In all my years of living, never before have I ever broke a bone, until menopause…I broke two! A lower estrogen level during menopause can lead to bone loss. This can cause bones to weaken, and break. So bone up(excuse the pun) on vitamin D and calcium. There's no need for you not to stay active and sport them stilettos. You're no where near the shawl and rocking chair set, but ask your doctor if you need a bone density test *before* you break anything. You still want to lift them legs to his shoulders don't you?

Ok. See, that wasn't too bad. There's a bit more, but I don't want to overwhelm you. Just wanted to touch on a few subjects to get you started so you won't be in the dark. Don't be afraid to ask questions relating to your body with your Gynecologist, that's what she's there for. If you don't have one, ask yo gurrl if she knows of one.

Just with anything new and different, menopause can be a pleasant rewarding experience. It's a rite of passage **earned.** No periods, and no more cramps! No more Kotex, tampons, no more pregnancy scares! Think of all the money you'll save in Midol and EPT alone! And no PMS in sight! No more soiled panties, so break out them sexy white satin sheets *anytime* you wild cat sexy beast*. Sex every day of the week…like a man. I am taking better care of me. Feeling stronger and more confident…like a man. I can do whatever I set out to do…like a man. I am not some mealy mouth pussy afraid to speak up for me. I'm a well adjusted Alpha personality, proud and aggressive. No longer will I be your demure wallflower standing on the sidelines watching as the world go by. There's a new sheriff in town dammit. I *know* there's a game going on, and I came to *win!*

Say it loud baby! **I *AM* KANG BITCH!** Keep your balls, I've got my own!

Damn! You just grew a brand new pair of BIG ONES! Ain't it funnnnn being a woman!

CHAPTER TEN

THE REALM

My dear Queen. It has been a long and arduous road, you have worked hard and therefore are now worthy. I am here at your beckon call, in book form to reference, guide and to do your bidding, whenever and wherever needed. I am your ace in the hole, your confidant, your first and last call when you're in a bind, your designated driver on life's road to success. You will come to know in the very near future, from here on out, all others **must** and **will** bow down.

Reclaim your throne. Your Majesty, I salute you!

Although this office does not come with an actual crown, cape and scepter, virtual ones will be awarded to you. Your crown, is encrusted with rare exotic gems in vibrant colors of the rainbow across many lands. It represents YOU, the beautiful eclectic mix of today's woman, the embodiment of wisdom. Your cape, is the newly acquired wardrobe, for protection from opposition. Sadly, more often than not, you're arrival is not always greeted by open arms. The scepter, are your finely honed red nails to tap and show when we are **NOT** amused. Enjoy, and wear them well my Queen. Wear them well.

As with all appointments with such a high caliber of power, use it wisely. This particular office comes with many glorious perks and fine trappings that can easily sway. Rule with a "Queen Bee" mentality, you'll have the **power,** but rule alone. Self knowledge. Self reverence. Self control. Three key factors to keep in mind. Practice being elegant, refine and charming. Be worthy of respect, uphold your value.

Interacting with everyone is all about being elegant, refined and charming. It shows you are a mature adult intelligent woman who makes an effort to be friendly. Don't argue or knit-pick about every little thing. Remember, when out in public, no potty mouth dammit! Be real with yourself. Your fellow subjects, potential clients and I, are counting on you. Test your embryonic ideas thoroughly before letting them lose on the general public. Keep in mind the greatest crime of all, Character Assentation. Offering up outlandish suggestions or wild hair schemes and plans without tried and true results, will only backfire in your face. A refined woman has impeccable table manners. The only thing that should be falling from your mouth is the art of the deal, not an orange peal! Being worthy of respect requires you to follow a code of honor. You earn respect by your words and actions, don't make someone else suffer gratuitously. Just because you are a **KANG BITCH**, don't act like a bitch letting your ego get the best of you. Our Queen is humble. Self knowledge. Cognizant of self. Repeat to yourself: I am in control of all situations. I am in control of *me.*

When you reach a crossroad, or are unsure of what to do, this **does not** mean you are indecisive. It only means a decision has not been made…yet.

First, clear your mind and breath. It may seem there's only one course of action to take but, second, consider if time is one of them. If time is not an issue, refrain from brainstorming, write down every idea. Ask for assistance from coworkers or others on the project. Just remember, it's *your* ass that is on the line, so keep that in mind when you draw someone else in. Certain risks must be calculated. Mistakes can be made, or can have a negative outcome so weigh the options, and make your decision from there. If time is of the essence, visualize the outcome in detail best/worse scenario. Fast forward as if you've already made the decision. Which one would you regret more? Make your choice. Good, bad or indifferent, stand by your decision. Be decisive.

Self reverence is having a high respect for one's character, having a high regard for yourself. Reverence has been defined as a strong sentiment of respect and esteem. Sublime or sacred. It does not necessarily imply love. Hell, I feel like that about a pair of Manolo's! Self control is controlling your emotions or behavior to obtain goals. In other words, don't buy the Manolo's...yet. Police your actions. Being compulsive, not reign in the desire to be bullish, and moving forward only to receive instant gratification can do you more harm than good.

Keep your emotions in check when dealing with others. We all become frustrated, but showing self control lets them know *you* are in control of you. At the office, if you find yourself losing your grip, smile, excuse yourself, go to the ladies room. Make sure **no one** is in there, throw some cool water on your face, or go to your car use a baby wipe. Breath deeply and collect yourself. Afterwards, fix makeup and hair. When you return to the meeting, **apologize** for the delay, NOTHING ELSE. Smile politely, then resume the meeting.

Uphold values. What do you believe in? What is important to you? Being truthful, being reliable or having credibility? To me, I'm all about being **truthful.** Remember the bath products? IT'S SOAP! Of course, it will clean my ass, so it's reliable! I could care less about its credibility. It's **soap**, it *will* clean my ass. No credibility issues here. Now here's the "got'cha" part. Who tested it? Based on what objective measurements? Any scientific field of research like biotechnology? The scorching rash was on my **CUPCAKE!!!!** I would rather someone slap me hard with their wet hand across my face than tell me a lie! Sorry, I *still* tend to ramble a bit, didn't mean to vent, still a sore subject with me. Annnywho, uphold your values, whatever is important to **you**. Moving on!

THE NEW ERECTION

Hope you are enjoying your new found stones! You know, a lot of men are going to have a problem the phrase 'Women with Power' and your aggressive attitude. But you know what I say...fuck 'em and feed 'em fish! They've had the balls, the swinging dicks, and all the power long enough. It's time to flip the script. The hunter now gets captured by the game! 'Women with Power' in the New Millennium are rewriting the 'Feminist Movement*' of the '60's. Unlike our predecessors, we now far out number our counterparts in the workforce. Because of technology, we are more willing and more intelligent enough to go all the way in order to achieve and have it all. With that in mind, we already know that sex is always on their brain. So, we'll make our new movement more palatable for them, with a playful twist on words. Since you have a shiny new pair of "Jewels", why not go for a complete set. It only stands to reason that you are now a strong independent self assured confident aggressive woman, and deserve new accessories to compliment your new found persona. With that said, I hereby bequeath you with a massive swinging one of your own! Unlike men, it won't be confined by an athletic supporter or jockstrap, because it doesn't need protection for fear of injury. The term, 'kicking 'em where it hurts', will become laughable to us. Or whip it out in showers to prove masculinity and sexual prowess. We don't have to reach a semi-hard or pull up our pants to show pride. Never more while speaking to anyone will the constant grabbing of the crotch to readjust the "boys" or scratch!

Why, *why* do they do this? I have noticed this when talking to men this happens all the time. They grab their nuts, in the middle of a conversation, readjust themselves, and continue talking!!! It is **the** most appalling thing a man can do while talking to a lady. More of that territory marking, boundary setting, tree pissin' bullshit. Well, we won't have to worry about that!

We only need to keep our 'imaginary member' inside our pretty little red panties next to our shiny new jewels to keep them company. It's a match set. You know how women *love* a match set. Like shoes and purse. Nails and lipstick. Woman with Power(smile). A chastity belt is no longer needed because *my* little cupcake is to be used at *my* digression. My sexual prowess is displayed by my femininity and strength. There will be no territory marking or boundary setting because my knowledge will be passed on to future sisters. Being an intelligent woman, I've learned to share, and that Each One *Can* Teach One. As for pissin' on trees. That's why God made rain.

Women with Power is not a far fetch nor a novel idea. Female rulers have reigned supreme back to the day of The Pharaohs. Legendary Queens adorned in the finest silks and drenched in exotic perfumed oils and priceless jewels. The Amazon Queen Myrine. Cleopatra. The last Pharaoh of Egypt. Nefertiti. Her captivating looks was unsurpassed and considered the lands most beautiful woman. Zenobia. She defied the Romans, but they were forced to pay her homage.

Those who disobeyed this mighty power, were beheaded by a simply wave of her lavish gold encrusted bejeweled hands, or sent into the lions den to fight for her amusement. Now, we're not going to off any heads, or send the men kicking and screaming into the lions den but, it must've been good to be Queen!

Please let me reiterate. I am *not* male bashing or saying we can get along without men. I want men to get along with us better, but they have a hard time doing this. If they could let loose of just *some* of the power, you will find we can live a more harmonious life. Of course that's not going to happen so…moving on!

You don't have to be an Amazon Queen or a Legendary Queen to rule Kingdoms. You simply must have the attributes of that Legendary Power. We have many women with that Legendary Power in the present day also. There are two that are uppermost in my mind. One, is my sista-woman, my "shero" our First Lady. The elegant, refined, sophisticated Mrs. Michelle Obama. Although not a ruler per say, she **rules** nonetheless. The wife of the first African American President and Leader of the free World, President Barack Obama. What an ultimate task and pure joy it must be to walk a mile in her shoes! The other, is the first African American woman to run a major U.S. corporation, Ms. Ursula Barnes, Chairman and CEO of the Xerox Corporation. Kudos to you my Queen! Knowing this, living now in this day and age, not only I am proud to be an American, I'm proud to be a woman!

Do you feel that crisp subtle breeze? That's me sweets, **KANG BITCH!**, whipping out my lace tablecloth!

Give the *same* word, a different meaning. As I said before, I like words, all words. Like men, I like to play with them, decipher them, take them apart. The first wave of the Feminist Movement began in the late nineteen hundreds. The Second wave, which is the one I am concerned with, because it focuses on the black woman, was at the end of World War ll. Not protected by North American laws, under paid, overworked, subservient to *all* men and used only as domestic workers. Thank you Jesus, that's all behind us now! There's a whole new movement on the horizon now.

This one is NEW and IMPROVED. Like that? I kneeeew you would!

THE NEW ERECTION. Women with power, stand tall. You don't need a penis to *feel* powerful! Now that's a mouthful. It'll scare a nice stiff one into a limp noodle. Well hell, if he's intimidated by a powerful woman, then that's not the man for me, you'd say. So true, but sometimes a woman with power can set the bar too high for a mere mortal man. Trust, the higher *up* the scale you move, the *lower* the pickings for quality males. I'm not saying to lower your standards, but open your eyes to new and different prospects. A hard man is good to find...uh, I mean, I *good* man is *hard* to find, so broaden your scope to ones you may not have considered. Improvise. THE NEW ERECTION consist of pleasing oneself. Taking care of your needs **before** meeting the needs of others. *You* are the most important person and are often, the most over looked. We have become our *own* enablers without even knowing it. We leave ourselves open to be venerable. Did you know the strongest always needs the most care? We take care of home, family, and if there's enough time, we take care of us…maybe. More and more we tire from being unappreciated by them, when all we have to do is **stop**. **Stop** accepting this behavior. **Stop** accepting it from them. **Stop** accepting it from ourselves. **Stop** it now!

My ultimate goal is to keep **me** happy. I spoil the *hell* out of **me**!

That's what I always tell myself. And you know what, I mean it! Sound conceded? Not really. Sounds like a **KANG BITCH!** graduate to me…and by now, it should be you also. If you are not happy with yourself, how in the hell are you going to make anyone else happy? You've heard that over and over again. But do you *listen?* It's all about you Boo, it's all about **you**. Always has been, always will be. We do so much for the people around us, that we forget about the most important person that is near and dear to us. I have eluded to it throughout the book. Need another hint? The Head Honcho. You. **KANG BITCH!** Yes baby Boo, it's all 'bout you. Inside The Realm you are a First Class citizen. You, are second to no one. The Realm is where you shine. You, are Numero Uno. Together we are strong, together we are confident, and very passionate when showing compassion. As a humble, intelligent woman, you stand beside your mothers, daughters, grand-daughters, great grand-daughters, sisters, aunts, cousins, as we stand by you. Share with those who are unaware, and teach the knowledge you've learned, then pass it on to generations so they will in turn pass it on. And so on, and so on. As a graduate of **KBU**, Each One, *Can* Teach One in order to achieve full capacity of life's enjoyment and pleasures. It is our true nature. It is the true nature of The Realm. It is the true new movement. Stand up. Stand tall. Stand straight. It is **THE NEW ERECTION!**

When most men think of a woman with power, they think of someone who is unapproachable, detached from the mainstream, or worse, an ice cold bitch. We're going to change that. Being a woman with power will mean having it all. Basically what I'm saying is don't make your career an end-all beat-all in life. Find a mate. Not to **complete** you(that's stupid)but to achieve *complete fulfillment*. Adam and Eve, Eve and Eve, Adam and Steve(hey I don't judge) match or mate find a partner. Finding the perfect mate can be easy, depending where you set the bar.

> Before I go any further, let me explain why that's stupid. You are already a **complete** person. That little miracle was taken care of by God inside your mother's womb. No one can do a better job than He. Got it? Moving on!

Only like 'em six feet and over? Honey, they are all the same length laying down. Fancy olive toned skin? Ever heard of nude sun bathing a day at the beach or bronzers? Is your potential hunk-a-hunk-of-burning love a little too Cro-Magnon? Schedule a spa day for the both of you. Keeping your emotions in check, make sure he has a female tech to do the waxing/laser hair removal so it will be more enjoyable and less tense for him. *You*, an Executive, *he's* not. Now, I can offer up countless platitudes on how opposites attract, but that's not what we're here to do. It depends on how much else you have in common, but you shouldn't dispel the idea of a romance because of professions. What you need to do is ask the hard questions *if* you're working towards a relationship. Will they meet your needs and will you be able to grow with this person across the board? By the way, regardless to what you've heard, opposites(in people)**do not** attract. **Like minds** attract. When finding a partner, the outer package or profession is never an issue. It's only one if you make it one. Ever see an obvious opposite but happy couple, walking hand and hand, seemingly so much in love, and wonder, what's the attraction? **Like minds.** Similar tastes, desires, wants and needs! They found their key to harmonious living. Look, the thing is, we are all damaged goods in some form or another with trails and tribulations. We've brushed ourselves off and are now standing tall, but some of us have not made the transition quite yet. Give them time, they'll get there, with a little help from a woman in the *know*. Living harmoniously is what it's all about.

You need to have someone there to share the load, the daily grinds, mishaps, ups and downs that are heaped upon your now competent shoulders. To be there to give an occasional bath or back rub and ease away the days tension. An understanding ear to listen when no one else cares. Comforting arms to find solace when your world goes wild. Even a Queen needs her down time. Make best of this together time to reacquaint with each other. I'm not talking about full-on hot and heavy, sweaty bodies heaving to the rhythm straight-up fucking, I'm talking about releasing pinned up stress*. There *is* more than **one** way you know! Talk to each other about the things that are bugging you. Find a happy medium on how to accomplish a solution, then solve it **before** moving forward. Once you get the heavy issues out the way, draw a bath for both of you. While there, talk about silly stuff. Make jokes, be playful get some water guns and have a shoot 'em out in the bathtub. Have a lazy Sunday picnic in bed complete with mimosas. Ooooo! If you're really feeling adventurous, go to brunch! You *know* how mother loves to brunch!! Make plans for future vacations or a simple easy breezy weekend jaunt. Go ahead have fun, enjoy yourself. Revel in each other! You deserve it. We work hard for what we try to obtain, and in the process we lose the objective. We say, I've got to save money for this, or I've got to diet for that. Keep this up, and you're going to work yourself up into a good lather, or what I call it a blue funk. You deserve a break from all the powers that be.

This is an appointment you **<u>cannot</u>** break*! Once a month, without fail, I want you to find *your* Nirvana*. Mark your calendar, clear your schedule. Find some soft comfy clothes and shoes, throw caution to the wind and go crazy! Uh, remember if you **leave** the house….you know. For the whole day, do something that makes only **you** happy. Tell the gang you're taking the day off, and if it's not bleeding or on fire, don't fuckin' call. Put the cell on vibrate. Go to the mall, buy a silly do-dad* or try a fresh new fragrance. Have a spa day, get a massage, have someone rub you the right way for a change. Try out a new do you've been wanting, get your nails done, or stay home soak in the tub, scratch your ass or watch TV. Do whatever pleases **you** without interruptions from anyone. Recharge the old battery so you will be ready to face another day fresh and on point, ready to read any son of a bitch if they have the audacity to displease this Queen!

There's a lot of self-help books on shelves about how to deal with relationships, manage your lives and how to cope with disappointments. All are good and I'm not knocking them but, I don't know, there's something missing. They hit the nail on the head, but didn't hammer it all the way in. It's like eating a meal, but it still leaves you a little hungry for more. They got to the meat of the problem, but didn't give you any gravy. The presentation was good, but did not appease your appetite. I want you to have full stomachs and greasy mouths when you push your ass back from my table.

With this lesson, I hope to provide you with a more *hands on** way of looking at the problems we face. In other words, I'm gonna give you some hot butta biscuits to sop up the gravy!

CHAPTER ELEVEN

THE FOUNDATION

Passion. A feeling that covers a vast emotional spectrum. One can have passion for another person, that can go from deep* I can't do without you love, to strong sexual desire, to white hot* scratch your eyes out rage! Or, it can be a passion for inanimate objects like hobbies or jobs. Passion. An emotion we haven't covered, but being a romantic, it's my favorite feeling, so we *will* cover it **well**! Passion is provocative, compelling, it evokes intense emotions, leaps and boundless enthusiasm. It hits me where my heart lives and breathes. Passion shakes me, quakes me to my core, leaves me breathless, wanting more. Some people love easily, wear their heart on their sleeve where it's easily accessible, I'm one of them. Not a hopeless romantic, but a *hopeful* one. Here lately, I tend to go into a relationship hoping this maybe could be the one, only to be left disappointed. Enter into another, with the same results, and the same outcome. Since I am **KANG BITCH!**, and did not want to become jaded, I had to take a long hard look at myself. Why was I *now* picking the wrong man? Was it me? Was it them? I wanted to find my Mr. Wonderful, but the guide I'd used for years for choosing a man had gone hay-wired somehow. These relationships had one common denominator. Me. I had to find something that works for *me*, because my damn "picker" was off. I was going off the deep end and sinking fast. What I needed was to step back from the situation, relax and breath because I was making too many mistakes. I needed some self control, to curb my fire and desire. I was looking in all the wrong places trying to please everyone else, when all I needed was to begin at the source. First, I had to do some reconstruction on my estate.

You've heard the old saying about, trying to please all the people all the time, well that's what I was trying to do. I'm here to tell you, it can't be done! You'll drive yourself crazy, go mad, and burn yourself out. That's a problem with Alpha personalities, we are **very** passionate when it comes to pleasing, and when it comes to a mate, we tend to go overboard. In business the same applies, we are so passion bound, the effects of intrinsic and external motivations over takes us. The foundation. We'll begin the reconstruction in Le Boudoir.

The Mistress Suite. We spend the majority of our time in bed sleeping. A poufy comforter, cotton bed sheet set, a couple of fluffy pillows will suffice and we're off to tra-la land. But, for the erotic times, or when you have given someone the pleasure of your company for the evening, your bed chamber should reflect who you are. Wild temptress, impetuous or demure, this is your playground, and it doesn't have to always involve full on sex. Maybe just some quite time for yourself, so make it enjoyable. You don't have to spend an arm and a leg to create a sexy boudoir. A few scented candles or incense here and there, a red or pink light bulb in a bed side lamp, a large throw pillow for the bed to prop underneath your hips*, just in case the mood changes. Before bed, draw yourself a nice soothing bath.

Complete the experience with a fragrant bath oil(no bath crystals!) sponges, loofas, a plush towel for drying off, and a bottle of your favorite aperitif in an exquisite cut crystal glass. Pleasant dreams Queen!

My Estate. The body that housed my essence was in need of some serious repair. I looked around my 'house' and was shocked at what I saw. My once beautiful sprawling estate, with a beautiful manicured lawn* was now in the shadows of her once former glory. My 'house' had become weak* and lethargic. My 'house' deserves better, I deserve better. Time for some remodeling. In order to build a house, you need a strong foundation for it to stand. Weight bearing walls* to secure it's roof. Paintings*, furniture and a beautiful manicured* landscape with a waterfall* on the front lawn. Then I'll be ready to receive company in no time!

Start with Kegel exercises. Kegel exercises is a way of strengthen the pelvic walls. Due to pregnancy and delivery, aging over time, the pelvic walls can weaken. Just like we exercise our bodies and muscles to strengthen them, we need to do the same for our little cupcake. To do the kegel exercise, think of it as cutting off the flow of urine while using the toilet. Squeeze these muscles tightly for a second or two then release. Squeeze, then release. Squeeze, release. You can do this while sitting, standing or lying down whenever you think about it, but do it throughout the day to reap the full benefits. It will strengthen the walls of your vagina, and make sex more pleasurable. Here's a tip. Although this may not elevate the problem completely, it will greatly help my Queens that suffer with incontinence. Ever seen any Rubenesque paintings? Beautiful nude buxom women laying casually on a daybed, eating grapes without a care in the world…and not a stich of hair anywhere! MOW THE LAWN! You know men hate looking for anything and they won't ask for directions. How are they going to find the button* if you're hiding it? Is it a fuckin' secret? Don't want 'em to know it's there? Trim back that hairy shit. Shave it, wax it, clip it, whatever. Get a mirror. Take your time. Go slow.

Stress. We are all guilty of instant gratification, we want it yesterday. We can be some resilient, ball busters when the need arises, but slow your roll, pump your breaks, take a chill pill. Don't over extend yourself. It can sneak up on you like a thief in the night, rob you of your energy, and zap you of your strength! It disrupts balance in the body and it's function. We try to deal with it in our daily lives, but there it is, staring us in the face. We need some stress busting remedies! Friends to tell you how they handle stress, opting for methods like alternative therapies, stress management, psychotherapists, depression aversion, yoga, shit get a grip! All you need is a little home grown common sense. Do whatever you need to do to relieve stress. A warm bath filled with aromatics and something nice and soothing to sip, a day at the spa or an outing with yo gurrls. Pay close attention. Are you ready? Ok, here we go, *slow it down!* Remember, it's all about you Boo, it's all about *you*.

A **KANG BITCH!** must always manage her stress* levels. Have some **me** time, alone with your thoughts to work things out, think things through. If you're really feeling frisky, how about a little self pleasure? Autoeroticism. Are you up for some solo sex? Masturbation. Oh, didn't know I was going to go there? How could you *not* know? I'm *the* illustrious **KANG BITCH!** baby! Don't get squeamish, we are all grown ass women here. We've had lessons on different subjects like flirting, the five senses, and we've touched on dealing with menopause and periods, etc.. It's only *natural* to cover this!

Men have used sleazy euphemisms like jerking off, cuming, playing with yourself, chokin' the chicken and what have you, which has no place here. I'm going to snatch(excuse the pun)the covers off this hush-hush taboo subject women have been too afraid to discuss. I am going to demystify masturbation. Get to the meaty part. I am going to discuss the right terminology and teach techniques in order to achieve *complete* satisfaction.

Masturbation. Don't you just love, love the word? I do! This is just more of **you** being in control. I'm the master of the bed I'm on! You'd be surprise how many woman have not experienced an orgasm through masturbating because they think it's taboo! Well, my Queens won't become a part of those sad ass statistics. I told you I was going to give you a more "hands on" way of looking at things! So, sit back, relax and get ready to let go.

An "Afternoon Delight". Morning, noon, night, rain or shine, while the kids are at school, in the middle of a rinse cycle, whenever the mood strikes. It takes place at *you're* whim. That's the good thing about it. *You* are always in control of when, where it happens, and who participates, or not. A Queen only has to conjure one up*!

There's a lot of health benefits to masturbation. I said that because a lot of women have been made to feel guilty by society because we masturbate. Or, have been told something bad will happen if we do this horrible thing. Now aint *that* a bitch! Needless to say, unlike men were told as boys, masturbating will not make you go blind, grow fur on your hands, nor will you go mad if you do it too often. Bottom line, masturbating feels good and is very pleasurable. It is one of **the** most intense organism you will ever experience because **you** have the power and **you** are controlling it…. which is probably why they told us not to do it! Bastards!

Ironically, one of the questions my doctor asked when I went in for first my check up with her was," How is your sex life?" Since I was new to the area I said, "Non-existent, but I do masturbate." She laughed out loud, and commended me for my honesty saying, she wished more of her patients were as opened minded about their bodies as I was. That began a long conversation about masturbation as she said it can also lower blood pressure. There's a whole laundry list of health benefits to masturbating. If you're experiencing a low libido, masturbate. It improves your mood, the more orgasms, the better you feel. It lowers your risk for type -2 diabetes and above all, it relieves stress. Gurrl, it aint nothing like a satisfied Queen!

Masturbation can make you more aware and in tuned with yourself and your pleasure zones. It can be done by you, with a sex toy*, your fingers, with or without a partner, penetration or not. Don't you just love it? Finally, you're in *control!* For those who don't know, the search is over, the G spot can be found on the frontal walls as you enter the vagina just below the clitoris. The clit or button, is the main player. It's like a penis when we become aroused. It engorges with blood and becomes hard. We don't ejaculate like men of course, but secretes a clear fluid that oozes through the vaginal walls. That's why men refer to it as being juicy*. Although some women can find equal pleasure in other parts of the body once manipulated, this part of the woman's anatomy causes extreme pleasure when gently stimulated. Stroke it gently. Because it is so near to the clitoris, it shares the same membranes, so there's no need to enter the vagina completely to achieve organism. Just remember, you are in control, you are the dominate one. Masturbating will help you to have more control over your organisms. It will help you gain a better understanding of your body as to what pleases **you**.

When I told you to find *your* Nirvana, incorporate masturbating into one of the "appointment you **<u>cannot</u>** break". Watching a pornographic movie, while gently rubbing your clit, can elicit some delicious excitement for an Afternoon Delight alone in bed. Fantasize. You can either chose to have a partner or not, or conjure one up! Sometimes a mate is not available when you're in the mood, or you're a single Queen, and there's not a mate in the picture. For those times, you should know how to(*TCB*) *Take Care Business.* A woman don't always need a partner to be sexually fulfilled. If you do have a partner, pass this information on to them(Each One *Can* Teach One)so they too can be more in tuned with **you!**

Please note: Most flavored based lubricants are not intended for vaginal use.

Be sure to use a water based lubricant to intensify your pleasure with sex toys like dildos, vibrators, or Ben Wa balls. They can also be fun and add an enjoyable pleasure to your sexual play, but be very careful if it requires insertion. Toys can become embedded up there, and a trip to the ER is not my idea of a pleasant Afternoon Delight. Whips, chains, fuzzy handcuffs whatever your pleasure do it, but remember the Doctor's Hippocratic Oath: First, do no harm. If Miss Lucy is not juicy as she once was, masturbating can remedy that. Just *thinking* of completely satisfying yourself sexually will trigger endorphins in the brain. Miss Lucy will flow like a waterfall!

Who is that one you've longed for my Queen? They are here now for *your* pleasure. To do *your* bidding. *You* are in control. *You* have the power. Are you ready to begin?

Lie down. Fantasize.

Who's that beautiful sexy beast you've always wanted? You can have them you know, **you** can have *anyone* you want. They're here. Can you see them, **now** at your bed?

Hover over me like a cloud, caress my body. Starving lips left too long unkissed. My body throbs as I remember, swept away in my desire. Gently stroke my hair. Take me into a drunken ecstasy. Make my hard nipples dance in your mouth.

Your well educated tongue slowly running up and down my stomach, in and around and in between my full lusty thighs. From the pillow, lift my hips to your eager lips. Hunger for me. Taste my sweet wet honeypot. Suckle my clit like ripe peach as my juices quench your thirst for my passion. Feast on me as though I was your last meal, I brace for the thrill, my heart quickens as I reach ecstasy.

Part my legs. Let the waves of passion ripple across my body as you plunge deeply into my cove. Explode like thunder, rain into me. White hot flames burning within.

Go deeper, and then deeper still!! Do with me as you wish. No one is watching. Take me. Take all of me now!!!! Now!!! Yes! Yes!! Yes!!! Yes!!!!

WHEW!

Everybody still with me? Ok.

You can also make good use of bath time by using a good shower head. Aim it directly at your clit for a sensational, pulsating, delicious climax and wash the day's drama down the drain.

The 'house' in which your essence lies. The sprawling estate, with it's bountiful hills, deep valleys, and tight crevices should be kept well managed, and fully cared for with a manicured lawn at all times.

Masturbation. No longer taboo. A useful tool in the arsenal of a **KANG BITCH!** Take care of **you** first, so you can properly take care of others. Always make time for **you**, and always make time for An Afternoon Delight.

My Mr. Wonderful found his way into my life…and not a moment too soon!

CHAPTER TWELVE

IN CLOSING

Well my Queen, our first course, **KANG BITCH! #101**, has come to a close. Leave on a high note with 'em wanting for more, I always say. I've certainly enjoyed my time with you, and I hope you have enjoyed it too. It's been an absolute shear pleasure sharing some of my experiences. If I was too brash for some of you, tough! I'm **KANG BITCH!** baby, and by *now*, you should be saying it also. Woman up! This is a hard, tough world we live in, and the sooner you develop a thick skin, the sooner you will be successful. You now know, the price of success does not come cheap, nor does it come easy, but the end *does* justify the means. By having the balls to stand up for yourself and read opponents. Yes, the lessons were at times were difficult, and hard to swallow, but in the end, you persevered, and acquired the all important passion! We are all in this together, and together we will stand tall. We *will* control our emotions, and our bodies before trying to reach out to find it in others.

The key to success? **Me. I *control* the power.**

Least we forget the great women with power. Oprah Winfrey, Folorunsho Alakji and Ursula Burns. To a woman with style, grace, glamor and sophistication our First Lady, Mrs. Michelle Obama. To women with unbelievable gall and hutzpah, Whoopi Goldberg and Millie Jackson. To the